NO HASSLE!

*Taking the stress out
of work*

Sue Cartwright and Cary L. Cooper

CENTURY
BUSINESS

First published 1994
© Sue Cartwright and Cary L. Cooper

Sue Cartwright and Cary L. Cooper have asserted their
rights under the Copyright, Designs and Patents Act,
1988 to be identified as the authors of this work.

First published in the United Kingdom in 1994 by
Century Limited
Random House, 20 Vauxhall Bridge Road, London SW1V 2SA

Random House Australia (Pty) Limited
20 Alfred Street, Milsons Point, Sydney,
New South Wales 2061, Australia

Random House New Zealand Limited
18 Poland Road, Glenfield
Auckland 10, New Zealand

Random House South Africa (Pty) Limited
PO BOX 337, Bergvlei, South Africa

Random House UK Limited Reg. No. 954009

ISBN 0 7126 5772 X

Designed and Filmset by SX Composing Ltd, Rayleigh, Essex
Printed by Clays Ltd, St Ives plc

DEDICATION

For Ben, Kate and Christian from Sue

*For my closest friends Alan and Joanie Djamogly
from Cary*

Contents

CHAPTER I

Stress is a Four-Letter Word: What it means and what it costs

Introduction

During the 1980s, we had 'The Enterprise Culture', which helped to transform British industry at home and abroad. But, as we were to discover by the end of the decade, there was a substantial personal cost for many individual employees, both managers and shopfloor workers. This cost was captured by a single word, *stress*. Indeed, 'stress' has found as firm a place in our modern vocabularies as 'fast foods', 'junk bonds', and 'software packages'. We toss the term about casually to describe a wide range of aches and pains resulting from our hectic pace of work and domestic life: 'I really feel stressed,' someone says to describe a vague yet often acute sense of disquiet. 'She's under a lot of stress,' we say when trying to understand a colleague's irritability or forgetfulness. 'It's a high-stress job,' someone says, awarding an odd sort of prestige to his or her occupation. But to those whose ability to cope with day-to-day matters is at a crisis point, the concept of stress is no longer a casual one; for them, stress can be translated into a four-letter word, *pain*.

For business in the 1980s, stress in the workplace was ten times more costly than all the industrial relations disputes put together. In terms of sickness absence and premature death or retirement due to alcoholism, it cost the UK economy a staggering £2 billion per annum. In terms of heart disease in industry (the single biggest killer), the British Heart Foundation estimated that it cost the average UK company of 10,000 employees, for example, 73,000 lost working days each year, the death of 42 of its employees each year (between 35 and 64 years old) and lost productive value to its products or services of over £2.5 million annually – with 21% of all sickness absence in the UK due to stress-related heart disease.

For the 1990s, it is likely to get worse. Stress is primarily caused by the fundamentals of change, lack of control and high workload. The build-up and aftermath of the recession, the European community, increasing cross-national mergers, increasing international competition and joint ventures between organisations across boundaries will inevitably lead to a variety of corporate 're's': reorganisation, relocations of personnel, redesign of jobs and reallocation of roles and responsibilities. *Change* will be the password of the middle to late 1990s, with its accompanying job insecurities, corporate culture clashes and significantly different styles of managerial leadership, in other words, massive organisational change and the inevitable stress. In addition, this change will bring with it a larger scale workload, as companies try to create 'lean fighting machines' to compete in the European and international arenas. This will mean that there will be fewer people to do more work, which will put enormous pressure on existing employees.

And finally, as we move away from the UK and enter larger economic systems (the EC or some larger pan-European body), individual organisations will have less control over their business life. Rules and regulations will begin to be imposed in terms of labour laws, health and safety at work, methods of production, distribution and remuneration, and so on. All laudable issues of concern in their own right, but, nevertheless, workplace constraints which will inhibit individual control and autonomy. Without being too gloomy, we have in the 1990s, therefore, all the ingredients of corporate stress; an ever-increasing workload with a decreasing workforce, in a climate of rapid change, and with control over the means of production increasingly being taken over by pan-European bureaucracies, whether the EC or some larger unit in the longer term. It appears therefore that stress is here to stay, and is not just a bygone remnant of the entrepreneurial 1980s. The purpose of this book is to highlight those aspects of people's working lives likely to be problematic in the future, and what individuals might do to overcome them. Although a great deal has been written in recent years about the source of stress, less attention has been focused on what people can do about them. It is hoped that this book will attempt to redress this balance, while at the same time highlighting stressful work situations that we can begin to de-stress.

In this introductory chapter, we will attempt to define what stress is, what research over the last decade has shown are its primary sources, and the recent costs of stress to organisations. This will help to lay the foundations for the rest of the book, which will highlight the everyday stressors likely to impact on the manager and employee of the organisations of the 1990s and beyond, and the strategies that might be used to deal with them.

Defining Stress

Stress is a word derived from the Latin word *stringere*, meaning to draw tight, and was used in the seventeenth century to describe hardships, or affliction. During the late eighteenth century, stress denoted 'force, pressure, strain or strong effort', referring primarily to an individual, or to the individual's organs or mental powers (Hinkle, 1973).

Early definitions of strain and load used in physics and engineering eventually came to influence one concept of how stress affects individuals. Under this concept, external forces (load) are seen as exerting pressure upon an individual, producing strain. Proponents of this view indicate that we can measure the stress to which an individual is subjected in the same way we can measure physical strain on a machine or bridge or any physical object.

While this first concept looked at stress as an outside stimulus, a second concept defines stress as a person's response to a disturbance. As early as 1910, Sir William Osler explored the idea of stress and strain causing 'disease', when he saw a relationship between angina pectoris and a hectic pace of life. The idea that environmental forces could actually cause disease rather than just short-term ill effects, and that people have a natural tendency to resist such forces, was seen in the work of Walter B. Cannon in the 1930s. Cannon studied the effects of stress upon animals and people, and in particular studied the 'fight or flight' reaction. Through this reaction, people, as well as animals, will choose whether to stay and fight or try to escape when confronting extreme danger. Cannon observed that when his subjects experienced situations of cold, lack of oxygen, and excitement, he could detect physiological changes such as emergency adrenaline secretions. Cannon described these individuals as being 'under stress'.

One of the first scientific attempts to explain the process of stress-related illness was made in 1946 by Hans Selye, who described three stages an individual encounters in stressful situations:

1 **Alarm Reaction,** in which an initial phase of lowered resistance is followed by countershock, during which the individual's defence mechanisms become active;
2 **Resistance,** the stage of maximum adaptation and, hopefully, successful return to equilibrium for the individual. If, however, the stress agent continues or the defence mechanism does not work, he will move on to a third stage;
3 **Exhaustion,** when adaptive mechanisms collapse.

Critics of Selye's work say it ignores both the psychological impact of stress upon an individual, and the individual's ability to recognize stress and act in various ways to change his or her situation.

Newer and more comprehensive theories of stress emphasize the interaction between a person and his or her environment. Stress was described by researchers in the 1950s as a 'response to internal or external processes which reach those threshold levels that strain its physical and psychological integrative capacities to, or beyond, their limit' (Basowitz et al., 1955).

In the 1970s, Richard S. Lazarus of the University of California suggested that an individual's stress reaction 'depends on how the person interprets or appraises (consciously or unconsciously) the significance of a harmful, threatening or challenging event'. Lazarus's work disagrees with those who see stress simply as environmental pressure. Instead, 'the intensity of the stress experience is determined significantly by how well a person feels he/she can cope with an identified threat. If a person is unsure of his/her coping abilities, they are likely to feel helpless and overwhelmed' (Lazarus, 1976).

Similarly, Tom Cox of Nottingham University, in the late 1970s, rejected the idea of looking at stress as simply either environmental pressures or physiological responses. He and his fellow researchers suggested that stress can best be understood as 'part of a complex and dynamic system of transaction between the person and his environment'. Cox criticized the mechanical model of stress: 'Men and their organizations are not machines ... Stress has to be perceived or recognized by man. A machine, however, does not have to recognize the load or stress placed upon it' (Cox, 1978). By looking at stress as resulting from a misfit between an individual and his particular environment, we can begin to understand why one person seems to flourish in a certain setting, while another suffers. Tom Cummings and Cary Cooper have designed a way of understanding the stress process, which can be explained thus:

- Individuals, for the most part, try to keep their thoughts, emotions and relationships with the world in a 'steady state'.
- Each factor of a person's emotional and physical state has a 'range of stability', in which that person feels comfortable. On the other hand, when forces disrupt one of

these factors beyond the range of stability, the individual must act or cope to restore a feeling of comfort.

- An individual's behaviour aimed at maintaining a steady state makes up his 'adjustment process' or coping strategies.

Included in the above description of the stress process are the ideas described below.

A stress is any force that puts a psychological or physical factor beyond its range of stability, producing a strain within the individual. Knowledge that a stress is likely to occur constitutes a threat to the individual. A threat can cause a strain because of what it signifies to the person (Cummings & Cooper, 1979).

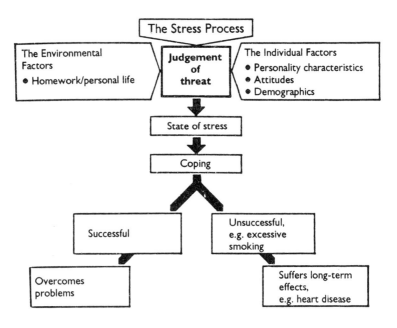

Figure I: The Stress Process

As can be seen, the idea of stress and its effects upon people has evolved from different research perspectives.

Figure 1 summarizes these different approaches into a general overview of the concept of stress.

The Biological Mechanisms of Stress

Stress is clearly part of the human condition. Because of its universal presence, stress is not looked at in terms of its presence or absence, but rather according to its degree and the effect it has upon individuals. Many of us seem to cope well with the pressures of work and family life encountered daily. But when and why is stress harmful to us? Consider what happens to the human body when it is subjected to a strain or pressure of some kind.

As Dr Andrew Melhuish, a physician specialising in stress-related illnesses, has suggested that man is the product of many thousands of years of evolution and for him/her to survive in a hostile environment required a quick physical response to danger. In other words, the body 'developed the ability to rev up' for a short time. This mobilization of forces is known as the 'fight or flight' reaction mentioned earlier. 'Primitive man expended this burst of energy and strength in physical activity, such as a life and death struggle with a predator' (Melhuish, 1978).

Modern man has retained his hormonal and chemical defence mechanisms through the centuries. But for the most part, our lifestyle today does not allow physical reaction to the stress agents we face. Attacking the Head, hitting the biology teacher who has refused to accept your overdue homework or smashing an empty automatic cash dispenser are not solutions allowed to today's society. Today, even the non-aggressive 'flight' reaction would hardly be judged appropriate in most situations. The student who walks out in the middle of an A-level exam, the teacher who flees from a rowdy class, or the assembly worker who dashes out in the middle of a shift, will likely suffer the consequences of their actions. Our long-evolved defence mechanisms prepare us for dramatic and rapid action, but find little outlet. The body's strong chemical and hormonal responses are then like frustrated politicians: all dressed up with nowhere to go.

It is this waste of our natural response to stress which may harm us. Although scientists do not fully understand this process, it is believed that our thought patterns regarding ourselves and the situations we are in trigger events within the two branches of our central nervous system, the 'sympathetic' and the 'para-sympathetic'. To paraphrase psychologist Karl Albrecht, 'in a situation of challenge, tension or pressure, the sympathetic nervous system comes into play and activates a virtual orchestra of hormone secretions. It is through this activation that the hypothalamus, when recognising a danger, triggers the pituitary gland. The pituitary releases hormones, causing the adrenal glands to intensify the output of adrenaline into the bloodstream. This adrenaline, along with corticosteroid hormones released through the same process, enhances one's level of arousal. All these stress chemicals stimulate the brain, nerves, heart and muscle to action.'

These physiological changes are designed to improve the individual's performance: blood supply to the brain is increased, initially improving judgement and decision-making; the heart speeds up, increasing blood supply to the muscles, and breathing rate and function improve; glucose and fats are released into the blood stream to provide additional energy. As part of these physical changes, blood pressure rises (as a result of increased cardiac output), and blood is drained from the stomach and intestines, as well as the skin, resulting in the cold hands and feet often associated with a nervous disposition (Albrecht, 1979).

While these changes are the result of the role of the sympathetic branch, the parasympathetic branch can induce a state of relaxation and tranquillity. As Albrecht notes, 'People who have spent much of their time in an over-anxious or tense state have difficulty in bringing into action the parasympathetic branch' and its helpful abilities.

All of the body's 'rev-up' activity is designed to improve performance. But if the stress which launches this activity

Table I: Effects of Stress on Bodily Functions

	Normal – Relaxed	Under Pressure	Acute Pressure	Chronic Pressure (Stress)
Brain	Blood supply normal	Blood supply increases	Thinks more clearly	Headaches and migraines, tremor and nervous tics
Mood	Happy	Serious	Increased concentration	Anxious and loses sense of humour
Saliva	Normal	Reduced	Reduced	Dry mouth, lump in throat
Muscles	Blood supply normal	Blood supply increases	Improved performance	Muscular tension and pain
Heart	Normal heart rate and blood pressure	Output rate and blood pressure increases	Improved performance	Hypertension and chest pain
Lungs	Normal respiration	Respiration rate increases	Improved performance	Coughs and asthma
Stomach	Normal blood supply and acid secretion	Blood supply decreases acid secretion increases	Reduced blood supply reduces digestion	Heartburn and indigestion giving ulcers
Bowels	Normal blood supply and bowel activity	Blood supply decreases motility increases	Reduced blood supply reduces digestion	Abdominal pain and diarrhoea
Bladder	Normal function	Frequent micturition	Increased nervous stimulation gives frequency	Frequency and prostatic symptoms
Sexual organs	(M) Normal sex (F) Normal periods, etc.	(M) Impotence (blood supply decreases) (F) Irregular periods	Decreased blood supply	(M) Impotence (F) Menstrual disorders
Skin	Healthy	Dry skin, blood supply decreases	Decreased blood supply	Dryness and rashes
Biochemistry	Normal, oxygen consumed, glucose and fats liberated	Oxygen consumption increases, glucose and fat consumption increases	More energy immediately available	Rapid tiredness

Source: A. Melhuish *Executive Health* (London: Business Books), 1978

continues unabated, researchers believe, the human body begins to weaken as it is bombarded by stimulation and stress-related chemicals. Many of the long-term effects of pressure are described by Andrew Melhuish in Table 1.

Stress and Heart Disease

Stress is also seen to play a part in disease related to lifestyle, where the degree to which a person eats, smokes, drinks alcohol and exercises plays a role. High blood pressure and heart disease are accepted now as having a proven link to stress. Hypertension, or raised blood pressure, in most cases has no obvious organic basis – it simply sets in. A majority of cases are diagnosed as 'essential hypertension', meaning they don't arise from any medically correctable function.

Although other factors such as diet, obesity and smoking surely play a role, many researchers now believe stress is the primary cause of hypertension. The connection, as Andrew Melhuish indicates, is as follows: hypertension is believed to result partially from changes in the resistance of the blood vessels. The diameter of the arterial vessels, which carry blood to the tissues, is partly controlled by the sympathetic nervous system and its release of chemicals through the vessels. Continual activation of the sympathetic nervous system's chemical response is believed to result in reduced elasticity of the arteries and raised blood pressure. This resulting hypertension can lead to heart disease because of the increased workload on the heart as it pushes blood out against a high arterial pressure. Also, high blood pressure increases the likelihood of a possibly fatal ruptured artery; the rupture of a vessel in the brain can cause stroke. Chronic stress, and its resulting release of fats into the blood stream during the 'fight or flight' response, is also believed to increase the risk of coronary heart disease by adding fatty deposits to the lining of the coronary arteries, which provide oxygen to the heart muscle. Malcolm Carruthers of the Positive Health Centre in London highlights the combination of factors that can result in a life-threatening crisis (Figure 2).

10

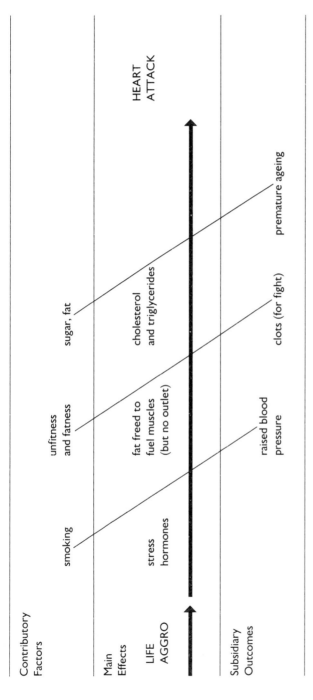

Contributory
Factors

Main
Effects

LIFE
AGGRO

Subsidiary
Outcomes

smoking

unfitness
and fatness

sugar, fat

HEART
ATTACK

stress
hormones

fat freed to
fuel muscles
(but no outlet)

cholesterol
and triglycerides

raised blood
pressure

clots (for fight)

premature ageing

LIFE AGGRO refers to life 'aggravation': stress agents at work, in the home, etc.

Figure 2: Flight Path to a Heart Attack
Source: an adaptation from Malcolm Carruthers, Positive Health Centre, London

Stress Costs

The costs of stress for the nation and for particular organizations are currently extremely high. For example, the British
Heart Foundation Coronary Prevention Group have calcu-
lated that 180,000 people die in the UK each year from
coronary heart disease, that is, 500 people a day. And that
heart disease accounts for 70 million lost working days each
year to industry and commerce. In addition, MIND estimates that between 30 and 40% of all sickness absence from
work is attributable to mental and emotional disturbance,
with another 40 million lost working days to the nation's
economy. The country has also suffered from increased rates
of suicide amongst the young, increasing by 30% from the
late 1970s to the early 1990s, particularly in the younger age
groups of employees. The instability and life stress have led
to divorce rates rising from 27,000 in 1961 to 155,000
divorces by 1988, and still rising. Indeed, Relate estimate
that by the year 2000 there will be four divorces in every
ten marriages. And finally, Alcohol Concern suggest that
alcohol misuse costs society over £2 billion per annum, with
an annual cost of alcohol-related absence alone at nearly £1
billion to industry. Indeed, they estimate that one in four
men in the UK drink more than the medically recommended
units per week and between eight and fourteen million days
are lost each year from alcohol-related problems, with 25%
of accidents at work involving intoxicated workers. So not
only is society in general suffering from stress, but also UK
Plc.

Who Pays the Costs?

Let's start at the beginning. Why is it that many countries
(e.g. US, Finland) seem to be showing declines in their levels
of stress-related illnesses (e.g. heart disease, alcoholism),
while the UK is still rising? Is it the case, for example, that
American employers are becoming more altruistic and

Behavioural and Physical Symptoms of Stress

To assess your own level of stress symptoms, indicate how often you have been troubled by the following behavioural and physical symptoms.

0 = Never or rarely
1 = Occasionally
2 = Frequently
3 = Always or nearly always

Behavioural Symptoms of Stress

Constant irritability with people	0	1	2	3
Difficulty in making decisions	0	1	2	3
Loss of sense of humour	0	1	2	3
Suppressed anger	0	1	2	3
Difficulty concentrating	0	1	2	3
Inability to finish one task before rushing into another	0	1	2	3
Feeling the target of other people's animosity	0	1	2	3
Feeling unable to cope	0	1	2	3
Wanting to cry at the smallest problem	0	1	2	3
Lack of interest in doing things after returning home from work	0	1	2	3
Waking up in the morning and feeling tired after an early night	0	1	2	3
Constant tiredness	0	1	2	3

Physical Symptoms of Stress

Lack of appetite	0	1	2	3
Craving for food when under pressure	0	1	2	3
Frequent indigestion or heartburn	0	1	2	3
Constipation or diarrhoea	0	1	2	3
Insomnia	0	1	2	3
Tendency to sweat for no good reason	0	1	2	3
Nervous twitches, nail biting, etc.	0	1	2	3
Headaches	0	1	2	3
Cramps and muscle spasms	0	1	2	3
Nausea	0	1	2	3
Breathlessness without exertion	0	1	2	3
Fainting spells	0	1	2	3
Impotency or frigidity	0	1	2	3
Eczema	0	1	2	3

Scoring: It is not the total score in each section which is important, but the number of either behavioural or physical symptoms on which you score 2 or 3. If, in either category, you are showing more than 3 symptoms with scores of 2 or 3, then it is indicative potentially of some current stress-related problem.

caring for their employees, and less concerned about 'the bottom line'. I'm afraid the answer is 'no'. Two trends in the US are forcing American firms to take action. First, American industry is facing an enormous and ever-spiralling bill for employee health-care costs. Individual insurance costs have risen by 50% over the past two decades, but the employers' contribution has risen by over 140%. It has also been estimated that over $700 million a year is spent by American employers to replace the 200,000 men aged 45 to 65 who die or are incapacitated by coronary artery disease alone. Top management at Xerox estimate that the cost of losing just one executive to a stress-related illness costs the organization $600,000. In the UK, however, employers can create intolerable levels of stress on their employees, and it's the taxpayer who picks up the bill, through the National Health Service. There is no direct accountability or incentive for firms to maintain the health of their employees. Of course, the indirect costs are enormous, but rarely does the firm actually attempt to estimate this cost; they treat absenteeism, labour turnover and even low productivity as an intrinsic part of running a business (Dale & Cooper, 1992).

Second, there is another source of growing costs, too. More and more employees, in American companies at least, are litigating against their employers, through the worker compensation regulations and laws, in respect of job-related stress, or what is being termed 'cumulative trauma'. For example, in California, the stress-related compensation claims for psychiatric injury now total over 3,000 a year, since the California Supreme Court upheld its first stress-disability case in the early 1970s. The California labour code now states specifically that workers' compensation is allowable for disability or illness caused by 'repetitive mentally or physically traumatic activities extending over a period of time, the combined effect of which causes any disability or need for medical treatment'. California may be first; but what happens there has a habit of reaching other places after a longer or shorter time-lapse (Ivancevich, Matteson & Richards, 1985).

In the UK, we are just beginning to see a move toward greater litigation by workers about their conditions of work. Several unions are supporting cases by individual workers, and the trend is certainly in the direction of future disability claims and general damages being awarded on the basis of 'stress at work', as Earnshaw & Cooper (1991) highlight in their work on workers' compensation and stress-related claims.

The stresses of work

During the 1980s, much of the research in the field of workplace stress suggested that there are six major sources of pressure at work (Cooper, Cooper & Eaker, 1988). Although we can find each of these implicated in an individual's stress profile or, indeed, in an organization's profile, these factors vary in the degree to which they are found to be causally linked to stress in a particular job or organization (Figure 3).

As a starting point to understanding work stress, researchers have studied those factors which may be intrinsic to the job itself, such as: working conditions; shift work; long hours; travel; risk and danger; new technology; work overload, and work underload.

Working conditions. Our physical surroundings – noise, lighting, smells and all the stimuli which bombard our senses – can affect our moods and overall mental state, whether or not we find them consciously objectionable (Cooper & Smith, 1985).

Each occupation has its own potential environmental sources of stress. For example, in jobs where individuals are dealing with close-detail work, poor lighting can create eyestrain. On the other hand, extremely bright lighting or glare can present problems for money-market dealers.

The design or physical setting of the workplace can be another potential source of stress. If an office is badly designed, with relevant personnel spread throughout a building, inadequate communication networks can develop, resulting in

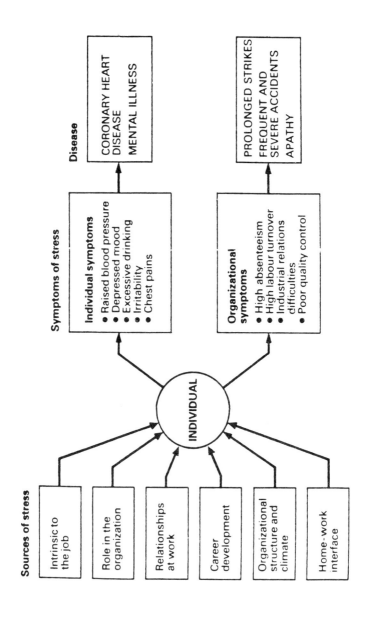

Figure 3: Dynamics of Work Stress
Source: Cooper, Cooper & Eaker. (1988). *Living with Stress*. London: Penguin Books.

role ambiguity and poor relationships. This problem is not restricted to offices. For example, one company found it had a high turnover and absenteeism among its mainly female assembly-line workers. When researchers looked into the problem, it was discovered that the women were isolated from each other due to the layout of conveyor belts used in the work. They felt bored and lonely working without human interaction. Once the assembly line was reorganized to put the women into groups, the absenteeism dropped substantially.

Shift Work. Many workers today have jobs requiring them to work in shifts, some of which go around the clock. Many studies have found that shift work is a common occupational stressor. It has even been determined that shift work affects blood temperature, metabolic rate, blood sugar levels, mental efficiency and work motivation, not to mention sleep patterns and family and social life. In one study of air-traffic controllers (Cobb & Rose, 1973), shift work was isolated as a major problem area, although other major job stressors were also present. These workers had four times the prevalence of hypertension, and also more mild diabetes and peptic ulcers than did a control group of second-class airmen.

Long hours. The long working hours required by many jobs appear to take a toll on employee health. Studies have established a link between long working hours and deaths due to coronary heart disease. In an investigation of light industrial workers in the US (Breslow & Buell, 1975), it was found that individuals under 45 years of age who worked more than 48 hours a week had twice the risk of death from coronary heart disease as did similar individuals working a maximum of 40 hours a week. Another study (Russek & Zohman, 1958) of 100 young coronary patients revealed that 25% of them had been working at two jobs, and an additional 40% worked for more than 60 hours a week. Many individuals, such as executives working long hours and medical residents who may have no sleep for 36 hours or more, may find that both they, and the quality of their work suffers. It is now commonly recognized that working beyond 40 to 50 hours a week results in time spent that is increasingly unproductive. Indeed, the EC's Social Charter has specifically attempted to limit Community countries to a 48-hour working week.

Travel. Although travel opportunities are appealing to many senior managers, travel also can be a source of stress. Traffic jams on the roads or at airports, delayed flights or trains, and the logistics of unknown places and people can present stressors as well as challenges. Marriages and families can suffer if one member spends significant time away. In addition, a travelling manager spends less time with fellow workers and may miss out on opportunities or feel out of step with 'office politics'.

New technology. The introduction of new technology into the work environment has required management and workers alike to continually adapt to new equipment, systems and ways of working. Having a boss trained in the 'old ways' may be an extra burden for the new employee trained in the latest methods, and raises questions about the adequacy of supervision and employee doubts about those in senior positions.

In a study investigating sources of stress among executives in ten countries (Cooper, 1984), Japanese executives suffered particularly from pressure to keep up with new technology, that is, to maintain their technological superiority. Managers in developing countries felt pressure due to the increasing emphasis on new technology, the need to deal with an inadequately trained workforce and the imposition of deadlines. Also, in Britain, a high percentage of executives (second only to Japan) indicated that 'keeping up with new technology' was a great source of pressure at work. This is not surprising in a nation that many people feel is beginning to slip behind competitors in the race to grab new export markets. In addition, these British managers described a high level of stress due to the amount of travel required by their work.

Work overload. Two different types of work overload have been described by researchers. 'Quantitative' overload refers simply to having too much work to do. 'Qualitative' overload refers to work that is too difficult for an individual. In the first case, too much work often leads to working long hours, with the attendant problems described above. A too-heavy work burden has also been connected with increased cigarette smoking, alcohol consumption and other stress indicators (French & Caplan, 1972).

Role in the organization
When a person's role in an organization is clearly defined and understood, and when expectations placed upon the individual are also clear and non-conflicting, stress can be kept to a minimum. But as researchers have clearly seen, this is not the case in many worksites. Three critical factors – role ambiguity, role conflict and the degree of responsibility for others – are seen to be major sources of stress (Ivancevich & Matteson, 1980).

Role ambiguity. Role ambiguity arises when an individual does not have a clear picture about his work objectives, his co-workers' expectations of him, and the scope and responsibilities of his job. Often this ambiguity results simply because a senior executive does not lay out to the individual exactly what his/her role is. The stress indicators found to relate to role ambiguity are depressed mood, lowered self-esteem, life dissatisfaction, low motivation to work and the intention to leave a job.

Role conflict. Role conflict exists when an individual is torn by conflicting job demands or by doing either things he or she does not really want to do or things which he or she does not believe are part of the job. Managers may often feel themselves torn between two groups of people who demand different types of behaviour or who believe the job entails different functions. As might be expected, studies have shown that people with high anxiety levels suffer more from role conflicts than do people who are more flexible in their approach to life (Quick & Quick, 1984).

Responsibility. Responsibility has been found to be another organizational role stressor. In an organization, there are basically two types of responsibility: responsibility for people, and responsibility for things, such as budgets, equipment and buildings. Responsibility for people has been found to be particularly stressful. Studies in the 1960s found that responsibility for people was far more likely to lead to coronary heart disease than was responsibility for things. Being responsible for people usually requires spending more time interacting with others, attending meetings and attempting to meet deadlines. An early investigation in the UK of 1,200 managers sent by their companies for annual medical examinations linked physical stress to age and level of responsibility (Pincherle, 1972). The older the executive and the more responsibility held by him, the greater the probability of coronary heart disease risk factors.

The stressful nature of having responsibility for others has grown in the economic climate of the 1990s, with so many industries facing cost-cutting exercises. As industries implement cutbacks in production and sales, managers are caught between the two goals of keeping personnel costs to a minimum and looking after the welfare of subordinates in terms of job security and stability.

Relationship at work

Other people – and our varied encounters with them – can be major sources of both stress and support. At work, especially, dealings with bosses, subordinates and colleagues can dramatically affect the way we feel at the end of the day. Hans Selye suggested that learning to live with other people is one of the most stressful aspects of life; 'good relationships between members of a group are a key factor in individual and organizational health'.

There are three critical relationships at work: relationships with superiors, relationships with subordinates and relationships with colleagues or co-workers.

Relationships with bosses. Physicians and clinical psychologists support the idea that problems of emotional disability often result when the relationship between a subordinate and a boss is psychologically unhealthy for one reason or another. A US study which focused on the relationship of workers to an immediate boss found that when the boss was perceived as considerate, there was 'friendship, mutual trust, respect and a certain warmth between boss and subordinate'. Workers who said their boss was low on consideration reported feeling more job pressure. Workers who were under pressure reported that their bosses did not give them criticism in a helpful way, played favourites and 'pulled rank and took advantage of them whenever they had got a chance' (Buck, 1972).

Relationships with subordinates. The way in which a manager supervises the work of others has always been considered a critical aspect of his or her work. For instance, the inability to delegate has been a common criticism levelled against some managers. Managerial stress may be particularly high for those individuals with technical and scientific backgrounds, which may be more things-oriented. For these managers, personal relationships may appear more trivial and time-consuming than for managers who are more people-oriented. This is particularly true of individuals promoted to management positions on the basis of their technical skills, without management training, who often encounter serious relationship problems at work.

Relationships with colleagues. Stress among co-workers can arise from the competition and personality conflicts usually described as 'office politics'. Adequate social support can be critical to the health and wellbeing of an individual and to the atmosphere and success of an organization. Because most people spend so much time at work, the relationships among co-workers can provide valuable support or, conversely, can be a huge source of stress.

A particular personality – that of the abrasive, hard-driving individual – has been seen to create stress for those around them. Harry Levinson of Harvard suggests that these abrasive people cause stress for other individuals because they ignore the interpersonal aspects of feelings and sensibilities of social interaction. The highly technical, achievement-oriented, hard-driving individual finds no time to consider working relationships and as such may be a source of interpersonal stress for others.

Career development

A host of issues can act as potential stressors throughout one's working life. The lack of job security; fear of job loss, obsolescence or retirement; and numerous performance appraisals can create pressure and strain. In addition, the frustration of having reached one's career ceiling, or having been over-promoted, can result in extreme stress.

Job security. For many workers, career progression is of overriding importance – by promotion, people earn not only money, but increased status and new challenges. In the early years at a job, the striving and ability required to deal with a rapidly changing environment is usually acknowledged by a company through monetary and promotional rewards. At middle age, however, many people find their career progress has slowed or stopped. Job opportunities may become fewer, available jobs can require longer to master, old knowledge may become obsolete, and energy levels can flag at the same time as younger competition is threatening. The fear of demotion or obsolescence can be strong for those who believe they will suffer some erosion of status before they retire.

Job performance. The process of being evaluated and appraised can be a stressful experience for all of us. It must be recognized that performance appraisals can be anxiety-provoking, for both the individual being examined and the person doing the judging and appraising. The supervisor making performance judgements faces the threat of union grievance procedures in some cases, as well as interpersonal strains and the responsibility of making decisions affecting another person's livelihood.

The way in which an evaluation is carried out can affect the degree of anxiety experienced. For example, taking a written examination can be a short-term stressor, while continuous and confidential appraisals by supervisors can have a more long-term effect, depending on the structure and climate of the organization.

Organizational structure and climate

Just being part of an organization can present threats to an individual's sense of freedom and autonomy. Organizational workers sometimes complain they do not have a sense of belonging, lack adequate opportunities to participate, feel their behaviour is unduly restricted and are not included in office communications and consultations.

As early as the 1940s, researchers began reporting that workers who were allowed more participation in decision-making produced more and had higher job satisfaction (Coch & French, 1948). As well, researchers found that non-participation at work was a significant predictor of strain and job-related stress. It was found to be related to overall poor health, escapist drinking, depression, low self-esteem, absenteeism and plans to leave work (Margolis, Kroes & Quinn, 1974). Participation in the decision-making process on the part of the individual may help increase his feeling of investment in the company's success, create a sense of belonging and improve communication channels within the organization. The resulting control, or sense of control that participation provides, seems vital for the wellbeing of all employees (Sauter, Hurrell & Cooper, 1989).

Home: work pressures

Another danger of the current economic situation is the effect that work pressures (such as fear of job loss, blocked ambition, work overload and so on) have on the families of employees. At the very best of times, young managers, for example, face the inevitable conflict between organizational and family demands during the early build-up of their careers. But during a crisis of the sort we are currently experiencing, the problems increase in geometrical proportions as individuals strive to cope with some of their basic economic and security needs. Individuals under normal circumstances find home a refuge from the competitive and demanding environment of work, a place where they can get support and comfort. However, when there is a career crisis (or stress from job insecurity, as many employees are now facing), the tensions the individuals bring with them into the family affect the spouse and home environment in a way that may not meet their 'sanctuary' expectations. It may be very difficult, for example, for the wife to provide the kind of supportive domestic scene her husband requires at a time when she is beginning to feel insecure, when she is worried about the family's economic, education, and social future.

Not only is it difficult for a housebound wife to support her breadwinning husband and at the same time cope with family demands, but increasingly women are seeking full-time careers themselves. According to the US Department of Labour, the typical American family, with a working husband, a homemaker wife and two children, now makes up only 7% of the nation's families. In fact, nearly 65% of all women in the UK now work, mostly full time. It is claimed by many psychologists and sociologists that dual-career family development is the primary culprit of the very large increase in the divorce rate over the last ten years in the United States and countries in Western Europe.

This dual career culture of the family particularly creates problems for women, since they are expected by men to work the 'double shift' – pursue a job and manage the home. Women, and society at large, are discovering the myth of the New Man, who seems to exist only in the wishful thinking of women's magazine journalists! The dual-career family also creates problems for men as well. For example, many managers and executives are expected, as part of their job, to be mobile, that is, to be readily available for job transfers, both within and between countries. Indeed, their promotional prospects depend wholly on availability and willingness to accept promotional moves. In the late 1980s and the 1990s, as women themselves began to pursue full-time careers as opposed to part-time jobs, the prospects of professional men being available for rapid deployment have decreased substantially. In the past, these men have, with few exceptions, accepted promotional moves almost without family discussion. Future such decisions will create major obstacles for both breadwinners in the family. We are already seeing this happen throughout Europe and the United States, and it is particularly exacerbated by the fact that corporations have not adapted to this changing social phenomenon. Few facilities are available in organizations to help either of the dual-career members of the family unit, particularly career break schemes (such as the recent Barclays Bank scheme) or flexible working years.

Plan of the book

The above stressors have been highlighted in research throughout the 1980s, and organizations have introduced global changes to attempt to deal with some of these issues, such as improving career development, redesigning jobs or providing counselling for interpersonal problems, etc. The approach of most books in this field, aimed at helping the individual to cope with stress, has focused on health-promoting activities, such as improved dietary habits, exercise programmes and relaxation techniques.

Whilst the health message is important and one we would strongly reinforce, comparatively little attention has been devoted to the more specific issues and situations which trouble managers and others at work and how to handle them practically. For example, issues such as dealing with interruptions, the everyday hassles of coping with new technology, dealing with the stresses of work travel, managing a bad relationship with a boss or colleague, making presentations, dealing with ineffective or debilitating meetings, etc. It

Daily Hassles at Work Scale

Could you please circle the number that best reflects the degree to which the particular statement is a source of stress for you at work.

	No stress at all		Stress		A great deal of stress	
1. Trouble with client/customer	0	1	2	3	4	5
2. Having to work late	0	1	2	3	4	5
3. Constant people interruptions	0	1	2	3	4	5
4. Trouble with boss	0	1	2	3	4	5
5. Deadlines and time pressures	0	1	2	3	4	5
6. Decision-making	0	1	2	3	4	5
7. Dealing with the bureaucracy at work	0	1	2	3	4	5
8. Technological breakdowns, e.g. computer	0	1	2	3	4	5
9. Trouble with work colleagues	0	1	2	3	4	5
10. Tasks associated with job not stimulating	0	1	2	3	4	5
11. Too much responsibility	0	1	2	3	4	5
12. Too many jobs to do at once	0	1	2	3	4	5
13. Telephone interruptions	0	1	2	3	4	5
14. Travelling to and from work	0	1	2	3	4	5
15. Travelling associated with job	0	1	2	3	4	5
16. Making mistakes	0	1	2	3	4	5
17. Conflict with organizational goals	0	1	2	3	4	5
18. Job interfering with home/family life	0	1	2	3	4	5
19. Can't cope with in-tray	0	1	2	3	4	5
20. Can't say 'No' to work	0	1	2	3	4	5
21. Not enough stimulating things to do	0	1	2	3	4	5
22. Too many meetings	0	1	2	3	4	5
23. Don't know where career going	0	1	2	3	4	5
24. Worried about job security	0	1	2	3	4	5
25. Spouse/partner not supportive about work	0	1	2	3	4	5
26. Family life adversely affecting work	0	1	2	3	4	5
27. Having to tell subordinates unpleasant things, e.g. the sack	0	1	2	3	4	5

is these everyday hassles that accumulate into 'real' stress outcomes, or, as the Americans term it, 'cumulative trauma at work'.

The rest of this book will highlight these everyday hassles, present some typical workplace scenarios and suggest some possible ways and techniques for dealing with them. Many of the hassles discussed emanate from fairly predictable everyday workplace occurrences, others concern more un-expected incidents such as redundancy, corporate takeover or sexual harassment.

The book is broadly structured into four parts; the in-dividual at work (Chapter 2), the individual as part of a work group (Chapter 3), the individual as part of the organization (Chapters 4 and 5), and the individual in a wider social context, i.e. as part of a family group (Chapter 6). In Chapter 2, we examine the everyday hassles which emanate directly from the desk or workstation and include issues such as time pressures, interruptions and work over-load. Chapter 3 considers the problems which arise from interactions with members of the immediate work group. In Chapters 4 and 5 we then move on to to discuss the every-day and more unexpected hassles which are characteristic of operating in a wider organizational context. Finally, Chapter 6 deals with the stressors and strains which emanate from the home/work interface and the hassles encountered in trying to balance home and worklife, such as the problem of dual-career conflicts.

This book is intended to be of interest to a wide range of occupational groups, particularly individuals with manage-rial responsibilities. Consequently, the situations we discuss are likely to be encountered by any male or female working in organizations. However, for purposes of style and clarity, it has been necessary from time to time to exclusively use the male pronoun(s). This decision was made on the basis that it is still generally the case that managers are male rather than female and does not reflect any gender bias on the part of the authors.

CHAPTER 2

Managing Your Desk

A lot of the problems we encounter both at work and in our personal lives we create ourselves. Typically, such problems occur because we failed to manage our time effectively; were unable to say 'no' and agreed to do something we didn't want to do or were unable to do in the time available; or because we totally mishandled a situation, upset others, lost control or got angry. The outcome of such situations frequently causes stress and anxiety and leaves us feeling bad or inadequate.

In this section, we focus on the numerous hassles that we are all likely to encounter during a day at work. Hassles which primarily emanate from our desk or work situation. Individually, these hassles may often appear trivial or insignificant to those around us, and when related to others frequently sound more like 'moans' than problems. However, their cumulative effect is often stressful, and they represent the type of hassles which can only be overcome and resolved by personal action. We will begin with travel, a major source of hassle that starts before we even get to work. Then we will move on to discuss time management, interruptions, managing workload and coping with new technology.

Travel Stress

'Travelling is the ruin of all happiness',
(Fanny Burney, 1833–1898)

7.30 a.m.

The day starts badly. You forgot to set the alarm and you're running late. You have an important client meeting at 9.30 a.m. and you intended to get into the office early to reread the papers in preparation for the meeting. You have to stop for petrol on the way in, which further delays you. Traffic is heavy and there are roadworks on the motorway. You find yourself in a tailback of slow-moving traffic and it's at least four miles until the next exit. As you're crawling along, you suddenly become aware that you have developed a flat tyre. You limp on to the hard shoulder and look at your watch. It's 8.50 a.m. and you're still some eight miles from your office. You're not going to make that meeting! What do you do?

Typical and ineffective response

You sit there fuming, then get out of the car and kick the tyre. Mentally, you set yourself up for a hassle-packed day by telling yourself, 'What a bloody awful day this has turned out to be . . . Why did *I* have to get a flat tyre today of all days?'

Effective stress-reducing response

You take a deep breath, calmly get out of the car and proceed to change the tyre. Rather than letting the situation wind you up by endowing an inanimate object, like the tyre, with the intelligence and malicious intent to develop a flat deliberately to delay you, you accept that whilst the timing is unfortunate, these things happen. As soon as you can, you call your office and explain the delay. You also ask your secretary to check your diary and try to put back or rearrange any later appointments. You ask yourself if there is anything you have learnt from the experience that could reduce the likelihood of it happening again.

After the weather, travel and its associated difficulties would probably rate as the most popular topic of conversation amongst the UK population. Getting from one place to another, whatever the mode of transport selected, often presents a major hassle. There are a multitude of factors which can potentially go wrong on any journey, and invariably do! Poor weather conditions, traffic congestion, roadworks, breakdowns, missed connections, long, often uninformed, periods spent waiting around at stations and airport terminals and jet lag all contrive to make travel a potentially exhausting and stressful experience. Travel, it has been said, broadens the mind; it is equally true that it can also blow the mind! Everyday work stress often begins before the individual has even reached his workplace.

There are many documented studies which have demonstrated that travel is stress-inducing and impairs job performance. For example, travellers crossing time zones at a rapid pace experience similar problems to shift workers, i.e. disturbed sleep and increased fatigue (Akersted, 1985). However, the focus of these studies has tended to be on travel as an occupation (e.g. pilots, bus drivers) rather than travel as a further dimension of work life more generally. One has only to spend a short time observing the behaviour of fellow travellers in an airport terminal or an M25 tailback, though, to recognize that one has entered a stressful environment.

Coping with travel stress

Car travel. In a recent unpublished survey of over 120 senior UK executives, it was found that whilst the car, not surprisingly, given its convenience and flexibility, was the most usual and most preferred mode of travel within the UK, it was also considered to be the most stressful. The executives considered that car journeys which lasted in excess of two and a half hours impaired their subsequent work performance. Apart from any effect on job performance, stress severely impairs driving behaviour in adversely affecting concentration and decision-making abilities. Drivers under stress are more likely to take risks, misjudge the speed of others or inaccurately estimate size and distance. Consequently, human factors play a major role in road accidents. According to the Department of Transport, fewer than 6% of motor accidents can be accounted for by road and/or vehicle conditions alone. Obviously, it is difficult to isolate whether travel is the primary causal source of stress or further exacerbates existing stress levels.

However, clear evidence (Cartwright, Cooper & Barron, 1993) as to the link between stress and accident involvement has emerged from a recent study of over 100 company car drivers. It was found that over a three-year period, drivers who were involved in accidents had significantly higher stress levels than their accident-free colleagues. Interestingly, accident involvement was found to be little influenced by driver age or annual mileage. Overall, the study also found that an important factor in predicting accident involvement was the extent to which individuals exercised time management skills as a means of coping with stress. In other words, the better or more developed the time management skills of the individual, the fewer accidents they incurred. This is because effective time managers are more likely to allow contingency time when planning journeys and arranging work schedules, and so are less likely to find themselves driving under time-urgent conditions when they are more prone to be careless and make mistakes.

Some organizations, such as Mobil Oil, ICI and Shell UK, run programmes and issue guidelines to help their managers avoid or cope more effectively with travel stress. ICI maintain that they have more fatalities through driving accidents than industrial incidents. Their advice to managers is to avoid travel whenever possible and to make fuller use of telephone and video conference facilities. If a journey is necessary, they suggest that where reasonably practicable rail or air services should be used in preference to travel by road. In addition, the following advice is likely to be useful:

In preparation

- Always allow contingency time when planning a journey, even if the journey is relatively short. Check out your route before you leave if you are travelling to unfamiliar areas. If possible, consult with others who make the journey regularly.

- Carry out regular maintenance checks on your vehicle. Discipline yourself to fill up with petrol, check oil, tyre pressure, etc. on your way home rather than leaving it until the morning; particularly if you have an early start, as many garages do not open before 8 a.m. Attending a basic car maintenance class can prove useful. Many local police stations organize special evenings for female drivers which provide basic car maintenance skills and advice on personal security.

- One of the major sources of stress associated with travel delays is the inability to contact others. Always carry spare change for parking meters and phone boxes, together with a phone card in the glove box. Car phones are invaluable when experiencing travel difficulties. If used with discretion, i.e. switched off when necessary, they can greatly alleviate travel stress. Of particular potential benefit to female travellers, many of the large motoring organizations will fit direct telephone helpline links relatively inexpensively. These enable the driver to summon help in the event of a breakdown; these organizations will also inform family, etc. of your delay.

- Do not be overzealous in the planning of your work schedules. Meetings invariably overrun rather than finish early.

In the scenario we presented at the beginning of this section, some advance planning and time management skills may have helped alleviate some stress, but what can one do to reduce anxiety during the course of travel, particularly if you find yourself stuck in traffic or waiting around for the breakdown truck?

Whilst travelling

- Take time to ensure that your seat is adjusted to a position which provides a comfortable body posture, and that your mirrors are in positions which provide you with good visibility without straining your neck. Such points should also be borne in mind when purchasing a vehicle; many Japanese cars, for example, were not ergonomically designed for drivers over six feet tall, although many have taken or are taking action to rectify this.
- When driving in slow-moving or stationary traffic, regularly perform simple relaxation techniques to reduce body tension; the neck, shoulders and hands are particularly vulnerable areas. Helen Frogatt and Paul Stamp in their book *Managing Pressure at Work* (1991) suggest the following exercise routine:

For the neck Slowly turn your head from side to side, then gently nod the head up and down.
For the shoulders Raise the shoulders gently to your ears. Hold and then let go. Relax, by feeling the weight of the arms pulling down.
For the hands Spread the fingers, stretch them out and relax. Then clench them into a fish and relax. Repeat this exercise several times.

There are are several relaxation tapes on the market specifically designed for use when driving. When selecting a relaxation tape, make sure that you listen to at least part of it before buying. For such tapes to achieve their objective, you must feel comfortable with the voice of the presenter, otherwise it will irritate rather than relax. Alternatively, you may wish to compile a tape of your own favourite pieces of music which have a calming and relaxing effect on you personally.

- Vary your speed to avoid fatigue. On long journeys, stop and take a short break to stretch your legs every hour and a half. Many motorway accidents occur because the driver momentarily nodded off; hot or poorly ventilated cars can induce fatigue.

■ Traffic delays and other travel hold-ups are particularly frustrating because they are events which are out of the individual's control. Aggressively thumping the steering wheel, cursing and sighing serve no useful purpose other than to heighten anxiety. Nothing can alter the fact that you are going to be late, so calm down, take deep breaths and find a more productive way of passing the time. Because it is recognized that Japanese drivers typically spend a considerable amount of time travelling short distances in heavily congested urban areas, Japanese manufacturers built into their cars a much wider range of sound systems and other gadgets than their European counterparts. These are deliberately intended to amuse and occupy drivers whilst in standing traffic. With some advance thought it should be possible to usefully occupy time should a delay occur, e.g. catching up on correspondence or making notes on a mini dictaphone, always carrying a reading file or using the time to learn a foreign language.

Rail and air travel. Much of the previous advice similarly applies to rail and air travel; however, here are a few additional tips:

■ Rail and air travel can provide a useful opportunity to catch up on sleep and arrive at one's destination alert and ready for business. Investment in a Walkman stereo can provide a means of replacing the facilities provided by the car stereo and can be used to play relaxation tapes to aid sleep. On certain long-haul flights, some carriers now incorporate relaxation programmes into their in-flight entertainment systems.
■ Many airlines provide general guidelines for air travellers. In particular, it is recommended that passengers limit their alcohol intake and wear loose-fitting, comfortable clothes whilst travelling. Though alcohol may have a temporary soporific effect, like coffee it is actually a stimulant.

■ It is recognized by airlines that the effects of jet lag and its disturbance to the body's circadian rhythm can be potentially disastrous to performance. Precise scientific formulae are used to calculate the necessary amount of rest time airline personnel must take before resuming duty. The effects of long-distance travel across time zones are particularly pronounced after westbound flight, in the afternoon and early evening – which is about the time the individual would normally have expected to rest. The speed of adjustment varies between individuals but recovery is generally faster after westbound than after eastbound flights.

Mobil Oil advise their executives that one day per time zone crossed should be taken to recover naturally. For eastbound flights, they suggest taking a night flight in order to arrive the following morning, staying awake until midmorning, then taking a nap of no more than two hours and afterwards remaining awake until normal bedtime. On westbound flights, individuals are advised to stay awake on arrival and not to go to bed until local time. Herbal teas and herbally derived sedatives can be useful in aiding sleep on initial arrival.

Managing Time

'All my possessions for a moment of time'
(Queen Elizabeth I's last words)

Assuming a typical response to the previous scenario, the day might continue as follows:-

9.45 a.m. You eventually arrive at your office, you go to collect the file for the client meeting and the phone rings. A subordinate is having some problems accessing information on the computer; brusquely you give hasty instructions. You then spend a further ten minutes wading through the huge piles of paper stacked on your desk, searching for the right file. You notice a new pile of correspondence and phone messages on the desk; some marked 'urgent'. You contemplate dealing with these but you're now already 30 minutes late for this meeting. Suddenly, you realize that before you left last night your boss popped in and suggested a meeting at 10.30 a.m. You're going to be late for that one too.

Typical and ineffective response

When an individual finds oneself in this situation, there is a strong temptation to cut one's losses, go home sick and abandon the day altogether, working on the premise that things are bound to get worse rather than better. One is reminded of the image of John Cleese as the headteacher in the film *Clockwise*, hurtling uncontrollably, yet predictably, from one disaster to another, with an imaginary key in his back which winds tighter and tighter, increasing his stress levels as he confronts each situation.

Effective stress-reducing response

Ignore the post, but quickly scan the urgent telephone messages. Delegate or get someone to phone back to let people know when you will be able to contact them. Have your meeting with your boss rearranged. Take a deep breath, relax and calmly go to the meeting.

Having taken the sting out of your immediate problems, you've bought yourself some time so you can focus all your attention on the meeting. Resolve to take time out to reorganize your desk as soon as possible – and do it! On your return, check everything is okay with that computing problem – it could result in repercussions.

Time, like money, is a limited resource which can be used to good or bad effect. However, whilst it is possible to make more money, unfortunately you can't knit more time – there can only ever be 24 hours in a day. The inability to manage time effectively is often a major source of stress. Whilst self-imposed time pressures can stimulate action, constantly working under time pressures over which we perceive ourselves to have little or no control – situations which we experience as demanding action yet giving us no time to think – are unlikely to result in good performance. Whilst we may blame others for wasting our time, the biggest culprit is usually ourselves. Time-wasters fall into the following categories:

The mañanas
Individuals who fall into this category cause themselves problems because they procrastinate; preferring to think about work rather than doing it. When things move on their desk, they don't leave it but rather they change location. Habitually, such individuals postpone decisions so that consequently tomorrow always becomes the busiest day of the week. When challenged, they invariably offer excuses for not having done something, rather than reasons. Whilst they frequently complain about interruptions, they actually often encourage them so that they can procrastinate even more.

Procrastination often stems from boredom, a lack of confidence or reluctance to seek clarification. As a result indecision becomes the safest option. Individuals also procrastinate when they are overwhelmed by work demands and are unable to prioritize the tasks in hand. Some basic tips to effective time management are:

■ Break up overwhelming tasks into smaller jobs. Set deadlines for completing the entire task and work on it a little bit every day.
■ Draw up a 'to do' list of all the tasks you need to complete in the short term (i.e. within the next week), the mid term (i.e. the next month) and the long term. Then each day draw up a list of things that you need to do

today. Regularly review your 'to do' lists and incorporate items on to them. Prioritize each task in terms of its urgency and importance. If you have difficulty prioritizing tasks, ask other interested parties to help. If you have agreed your priorities with your boss, he or she can hardly blame you if a non-priority item does not get completed today!

- When planning your work schedule, attempt to balance routine tasks with the more enjoyable jobs. It is a good idea to begin the day with an enjoyable job, then the sense of achievement will set you in a positive frame of mind for the rest of the day.
- Combat paper-shuffling by resolving to handle each piece of paper only once. Read it, act upon it, file it or throw it away.
- Accept that risks are inevitable and that no decisions are ever made on the basis of complete information. Set a time limit, gather as much information as possible and make a decision.

The poor delegators
Individuals who fall into this category waste a considerable amount of their time doing work which could easily and more effectively have been done by somebody else. Typically, this is because they lack trust in others, are trying to impress, fear confrontation or lack the ability to say 'no'. Poor delegators tend to expect perfection in themselves and others and often have difficulty separating the trivial from the important. If they do delegate, they worry and fuss and are unable to stand back; frequently checking up on others and changing instructions. Their interfering behaviour and overt lack of confidence in other's ability is often a major source of frustration to those with whom they work, and work relationships characteristically can be poor. They are prone to complain openly about the performance of colleagues and subordinates, yet they allow them little opportunity to develop. Rather than impressing their superiors by their indispensability, poor delegators often find themselves doing the

same job for years, because they have failed in their own development and that of those around them.

- Delegation does not mean abdication. Whilst initially it may take time to explain something or train another person to take on a new task, in the long term that investment will reap dividends.
- Always take time out to explain exactly what is required; poor delegators are often also poor communicators, which is why they are frequently disappointed with the efforts of others. Check at the time that the other person is clear about what they need to do and ask them if they anticipate any problems. Be specific as to when you require the task to be completed and indicate that they can come back to you if they need help or information.
- Having delegated a job, leave the person to get on with it. If you knew that someone was going to check everything you did, would you do it as well?
- As soon as you become aware that a deadline is unrealistic, renegotiate, delegate or let someone know. People are less upset and can readjust better if they are told some time in advance rather than at the last minute that their initial expectations are not going to be met.
- Avoid taking on unnecessary work that does not fulfil your objectives or could be done by others by learning to say 'no' politely and assertively. Practise saying it aloud in front of a mirror.

The disorganized

Individuals who fall into this category are instantly recognizable by the mounds of paper that form barricades around their desks. Disorganized individuals frequently miss or are late for appointments. When they do arrive, they have often forgotten or misplaced their papers and spend the first ten or fifteen minutes paper-shuffling in an attempt to catch up on what is going on. A large part of their day is typically spend in hide-and-seek-type activities; hunting for car keys, scraps of paper, cigarette packets with vital phone numbers on, etc.

Psychologically, disorganized individuals perceive their problems as stemming from work overload; they erect these barricades of files around their desks as a defence against the onslaught of further work. Whilst outwardly they give the impression of being immensely busy, they actually achieve very little. Furthermore, they tend to waste other people's time, as they regularly recheck details and instructions because they have initially failed to record such information accurately or have misplaced their notes.

Typically, such individuals subscribe to the view that creative minds are rarely tidy, rather than the more logical and likely explanation that a cluttered desk reflects a cluttered mind. Disorganized individuals are often anxious that their work contribution will not be recognized or are fearful that if they make things too easy for others to follow, this will in some way devalue their worth and may make their position vulnerable.

Here are some helpful hints for the disorganized:

- Remember that it takes time to plan effectively to save time. Setting up a system, colour-coding files for easier identification, investing in a yearly planner chart, Filofax, etc. to improve organization and allow you to regain control of your chaos all pay dividends in the long term.
- Discipline yourself to do the filing every day.
- Make out a 'to do' list regularly at the start of each day and review it each evening. Clear the top of your desk and put everything out of sight except for the task you are currently working on. Keep you in-tray somewhere else, e.g. on the top of a filing cabinet rather than on your desk. Then you will not be overwhelmed and demotivated by the amount of work you have to do.
- Stick to one task and finish it!
- Invest in a large hardbacked scribbler pad for recording all your notes, messages, etc. in one place, making a note of the date and action you have to take. Only photocopy material sufficient for your needs; avoid

making multiple copies for safety. Avoid spontaneous use of the telephone.

- Think before you telephone, draw up a list of *all* the information you require from the caller. This will avoid the necessity to call someone back several times as you become aware of further information you need as you work through the task. The open and closing courtesies of telephone calls all take up time. This will also save you time waiting for others to phone you back with information and you will be able to progress with the task without interruption.
- Identify your prime time for working, when your energy levels are high, for the complex tasks and save the trivial routine tasks for non prime time. Most people tend to be either 'larks' (i.e. at their best in the morning) or 'night owls' (i.e. at their best in the late afternoon/ evening). Research evidence suggests that larks tend to be more introvert and owls more extrovert personalities.
- Try to 'batch' phone calls or group trivial or routine tasks and tackle them as one task.
- When making an appointment in your diary, enter a finish time as well as a start time. Allocate time exclusively to yourself – to think, to plan, to write that urgent report. Don't fill up all your available time with meetings; just because there is a space in your diary does not mean that you are doing nothing and therefore that this time can automatically be committed to others.

The mushrooms

Individuals who fall into this category are usually unclear about the purposes, aims and objectives of what they are required to do. Rather like the mañanas they speculate and inwardly question what they should do rather than doing it. Frequently, they expend a great deal of effort performing jobs which are unnecessary, duplicate the work of others or do not match task requirements. Often they also waste time 'reinventing the wheel'. Typically, such individuals waste time because they are non-assertive, contemplating what action is required and remaining uninformed and in the dark, rather than speaking out and seeking clarification. Consequently, they frequently encounter difficulties in prioritizing and their behaviour can easily be interpreted by others as being apathetic.

Individuals who remain mushrooms are likely to become job-dissatisfied quickly. As their problem is basically a lack of assertion and communication skills, they are likely to benefit from interpersonal skills development courses. Many organizations run assertion training courses. Alternatively, many colleges of further education, extramural departments of universities, also run short courses in this area. Whilst there are a number of good books on the subject (e.g. *Assertiveness: A Positive Process*, by C. Beals, B. Hopson, and M. Scally, published by Mercury Business Paperbacks; *Developing Assertiveness*, by Anni Townend, published by Routledge), the key to developing assertiveness is to practise, practise, practise, and thus the opportunity to exercise techniques in role-play activities in a learning environment is extremely important. Fundamental to assertive behaviour is the acceptance of the individual that they have rights and responsibilities to others; numbers 6 and 7 below are of particular relevance to mushrooms:

1. I have the right to express my thoughts and opinions, even though they may be different from those of others.
2. I have the right to express my feelings and take responsibility for them.
3. I have the right to say 'yes' to people.
4. I have the right to change my mind without making excuses.
5. I have the right to make mistakes and to be responsible for them.
6. I have the right to say 'I don't know'.
7. I have the right to say 'I don't understand'.

8. I have the right to ask for what I want.
9. I have the right to say 'no' without feeling guilty.
10. I have the right to be respected by others, and to respect them.
11. I have the right to be listened to and taken seriously.
12. I have the right to be independent.
13. I have the right to be successful.
14. I have the right to choose not to assert myself.

(Adapted from Beals, Hopson & Scally, 1991; Townend, 1991)

Managing Interruptions

12.25 p.m. Having survived the client meeting and got through a rocky meeting with your disgruntled boss, who was clearly not impressed with your timekeeping, you arrive back at your desk. By skipping lunch, you may be able to salvage something of the day, so you turn your attention to that report which has to be finished today and which you planned to start two hours ago. You settle down to it, but you never get more than two sentences written before you are interrupted by the phone, or somebody calls by your office. Before you know it, it's 3.00 p.m. and you're still struggling with the first page. At this rate, you're going to be late home yet again tonight, and it's your six-year-old's school concert.

Typical and ineffective response You continue to battle through the interruptions, resign yourself to staying on late until it is finished and missing your child's concert, despite the inevitable row at home which will occur as a result. You produce a report with which you are far from satisfied and either take it home with you to rewrite over a bottle of whisky or worry about it all night.

Effective stress-reducing response Firstly, you take short half-hour lunch break and get some fresh air. Then you cocoon yourself in your office or move to an alternative quieter location to create an interruption-free environment for a hour or two in which to focus all your attention on the report. Consequently you are able to finish the report by 4.00 p.m. and, still have time to attend to your waiting phone messages, etc. organize yourself for the morning and leave on time.

It has been estimated that one hour of concentrated work is worth four hours of interrupted time. Interruptions take up time in themselves but they also disturb concentration, so that having dealt with the interruption, it then takes the individual further time to refocus on the original task. Telephone calls and casual 'droppers-by' are the two major sources of interruptions.

The telephone

Batching phone calls, planning what you are going to say or need to know in advance and deliberately disciplining yourself to place a specific time limit on the length of a phone call are useful techniques for managing the telephone more effectively. It is good practice to aim to limit telephone calls to three minutes. An egg timer by your phone is a useful device for going this. If the volume and complexity of the information you wish to convey is likely to take more than three minutes to transmit, then there are more appropriate means of communication available to you which are potentially less ambiguous and open to misunderstanding than the phone (e.g. electronic mail, fax machine, letter). They also have the advantage of providing an exact and permanent record of the communication for future reference. As many phone calls need to be reconfirmed in writing at some later point in time, a decision from the outset to use such alternative methods avoids unnecessary duplication of effort and time. It is also sound practice to check at the outset whether

the person you are calling has time to speak in order to ensure that you have their full attention. Individuals should develop the skill of terminating a call on an action point. When
making a difficult call which requires a positive and assertive
approach, handle the call standing up; this will help to reinforce your assertive behaviour and improve voice projection. However, whilst such tactics are useful in limiting
interruptions and using time more effectively, there are circumstances in which, because of their time urgency or
demands for creativity, it is necessary to get right away from
interruptions. In such circumstances, call-diversion facilities
and answering machines provide the solution. By way of an
experiment, North Western Mutual Life, an American insurance company, introduced a 'quiet hour' for their
employees, during which all incoming calls were blocked
and dealt with by the switchboard. Operators took messages
which were then relayed to employees at the end of the
hour. The scheme proved extremely successful. In one year,
the organization reported a 23% rise in productivity.

Casual 'droppers-by'

Whilst being interrupted can provide a welcome diversionary break from a boring or tedious task, too many interruptions during the course of the day are time-wasting,
distracting and irritating. For many years, fragmentation has
been recognized to be a key feature of a manager's typical
working day. The role of the manager is highly interactive. It
has been estimated that typically a manager will engage in
over a hundred brief interactions in the course of a day.
Consequently, he or she will rarely work for more than 30
minutes on any one item. To some extent, the problem of
interruptions has increased over the years as managers have
been encouraged to be more accessible to their staff and to
adopt an 'open-door' managerial style. Furthermore, changing attitudes towards work organization, the demands of
new technology and monetary pressure to use space more
efficiently have meant that open-plan offices, first introduced in the 1960s, have increasingly become the norm. The

debate concerning the relative merits of traditional versus open-plan offices still continues. A study of clerical employees in the USA (Oldham, 1985) found that employees experienced more difficulty in focusing on the task, felt less able to effectively communicate privately with others and were generally less satisfied with an open-plan layout than with more traditional partitioned offices. Therefore, whilst at a general/social level, open-plan offices may make it easier for individuals to interact, the lack of privacy and increased likelihood of interruptions suggests that organizations also need to provide quiet areas or designated rooms where employees can meet in private or occasionally work on tasks requiring uninterrupted concentration.

There are a variety of strategies for controlling interruptions:

- Establish quiet hours during which you can work undisturbed. This may mean closing your door and putting a notice outside. In open-plan offices, this is obviously not possible, although it is the practice in some organizations to encourage employees to indicate when they do not want to be disturbed. One such organization issues employees with a flagholder and two flags; one green, the other red. Employees place the green flag at the front corner of their desk when they are working on everyday tasks and can be interrupted. They display the red flag when they are working on difficult and complex assignments and do not wish to be disturbed. Providing such indicators are used sensibly, they are likely to be respected by others and so can be effective in circumventing some of the problems of working in open-plan offices.

- If possible, establish visiting hours when you are available for 'drop-in' visitors, and let people know when these are. Fix a definite time with others when you will answer their queries or review progress on a task, rather than leaving it open-ended.

- Whenever possible, arrange meetings away from your

desk/office; this enables you to take control and leave when you want to.

■ Do not think that it is necessary always to preface and end an interaction with an obligatory amount of small talk; a pleasant smile will often suffice.

■ Do not hesitate in curbing wafflers by asking them to make their main point(s) – if necessary interrupt them.

■ Do not invite casual droppers-in to sit down; this will encourage them to stay longer.

■ When unexpectedly interrupted, ask the person how much time they need, and if you haven't got it, explain and make arrangements to see them at an alternative time. If you only have ten minutes, tell them and be prepared to cut them short if they overrun that time. There is no need to feel guilty – you kept your side of the bargain. Pointedly looking at one's watch can be an effective strategy in getting people to come to the point or to recognize that you are busy and need to get on.

■ When it comes to interrupting others, practise what you preach. Think twice before you interrupt somebody else – do you genuinely need their input or are you just too lazy to think for yourself?

Avoid the automatic kneejerk reaction to pick up the phone or walk over to somebody's desk by preparing a list of the information you need to give or ask, add to it as you work through the day, and then see them once. Ask people if it is convenient to interrupt them and be sensitive and re-spectful of their time.

Finally, recognize that interruptions occur for a number of reasons. The person involved may:

1. want to exchange information
2. need reassurance or clarification about what they are doing
3. be too lazy or lack the confidence to think for them-selves – it is easier and less risky to be told what to do
4. want a casual chat to pass the time because they are

bored, haven't enough work to do or need the social contact
5. want to talk to you about something else, perhaps of a personal nature, but don't know how to initiate the discussion and so keep finding some other pretext to interrupt you.

Identifying the reason for the interruption can help guide the strategy for handling the situation and may indicate the need to change one's own behaviour or managerial style. For example, if you find yourself constantly interrupted by requests for further information and clarification this may suggest that your instructions are generally inadequate or poorly communicated. Taking time out to brief colleagues or subordinates comprehensively from the outset and encouraging them to ask questions and raise potentially difficult issues can often avoid a steady flow of subsequent interruptions. Similarly, the constant referral of trivial or minor decisions may indicate that you are creating or nurturing an overdependent relationship between yourself and others. As previously discussed, this may be because you are a poor delegator. Alternatively, it may be that people are frightened of you, or that you are too available and so may need to take action to sever the umbilical cord.

Managing Workload:
Working to Live or Living to Work

'I don't want to achieve immortality through my work
– I want to achieve it by not dying' (Woody Allen)

The impact of increased economic competition has in recent years led to substantial redundancies, downsizing and delayering within organizations. The organizational model of the 1990s is frequently described as being fitter, leaner and more hungry than its predecessor. Leaner and more hungry it may be, but whether it is fitter remains open to debate. Fewer people doing the same or more work means increased individual workloads and longer working hours. Meeting budget or exceeding productivity targets one year invariably has the result that, in real terms, budgets are cut and higher targets are set for the following year; working hard and meeting deadlines soon comes to mean working harder to meet even tighter deadlines the next time around.

It is therefore not surprising that work overload is one of the most commonly cited sources of workplace stress. As discussed in Chapter 1, work overload can be of a quantitative or qualitative nature. Working long hours to cope with overload is likely to lead to poor health and can also create conflict and resentment at home. As this will affect the quality of time spent with the family, it can lead to marital difficulties.

For many in managerial jobs, working long hours, either because of the perceived demands of the workload or because the culture of the organization dictates that working late is symbolic of an executive's commitment, has increasingly become the norm. Whilst the average weekly hours worked by blue-collar and manual workers has decreased over time as a result of industrial legislation, white-collar working hours have actually increased. For many managers, a ten-hour working day is not uncommon, despite mounting research evidence that working beyond 40 hours a week results in time spent that is increasingly unproductive.

Working women are particularly vulnerable to overload. Women often find themselves taking on too much work, on the basis that they have to be seen to be good at their job or be better than a male colleague in a similar position if they are to gain promotion. Furthermore, it is still the case that the bulk of the domestic chores and responsibilities of home, child-care arrangements, etc. fall on to the shoulders of the working woman rather than her male partner. The demands of these multiple roles, worker, mother, wife, mean that working women effectively have *two* jobs and can work as many hours at home as they do at the office or factory. Maintaining the 'superwoman' image has health costs. At a time when male smoking behaviour has been steadily decreasing, smoking amongst females has altered little and in some age groups has actually increased. Research has demonstrated that the incidence of coronary heart disease amongst working mothers rises as the size of the family increases, whereas, up to a certain limit, the reverse appears to apply to mothers who remain at home.

Too much work or personal inefficiency

If work overload is a major source of distress, then either you are not working effectively or you genuinely have too much work and need help from others. One way of systematically tackling the problem is to analyze how effectively you are working by keeping a time log for a week or two. To audit your time, divide each day into fifteen-minute segments, then at the end of each hour make a note of the activities you were involved in and how long you spent on them. At the end of the day, record the total hours worked during that day. Such details could be recorded in a desk diary or on a separate sheet of paper. John Adair, in his book, *Effective Time Management*, suggests that the following list of symbols may be useful in recording managerial activities (see page 51).

According to your profession or job, you may wish to devise your own set of symbols. For example, a university lecturer might include headings such as: Lecture Preparation, Marking, Teaching, Tutorials, Research, Pastoral Care, Meetings; whereas a GP might use the following headings: Seeing Patients, Seeing Medical Representatives, Writing Reports, Accounts and Budgeting, Home Visits, Practice Meetings, Reading Journals.

At the end of the week, this data can be summarized to identify the hours spent and the percentage of total time used under key headings.

This will help you to identify *whether* and *where* you are wasting time, i.e. the items which take up significant or unnecessary portions of your time but contribute nothing to your productivity, as well as areas where you could be better organized or perhaps delegate more. If the problem

Code	Activities	Notes (Time Spent)
C	*Committees* – any prearranged group meeting with or without an agenda	
I	*Interviews* – any prearranged conversation, formal or informal, with a purpose	
D	*Discussion* – talking not classified under C and I	
E	*Education* – participation in lectures, training courses, conferences and seminars	
F	*Figure Work*	
P	*On the telephone*	
S	*Dictating*	
W	*Writing*	
J	*Inspection* – a personal tour of the work place, walking the job	
Q	*Travelling* (and not doing other work listed above)	
T	*Thinking*	
O	*Others* – specify what they are	

Source: Adair, 1982

does lie in this area, it may be appropriate to reread the earlier sections of this chapter.

However, if the problem genuinely appears to be one of qualitative or quantitative overlaod, the time log will provide you with specific information that will help you present your case to others and negotiate for extra help. Initiating regular work group meetings to discuss current workload and task priorities, particularly if your workload emanates from several different sources, can be useful in gaining the support of others and sharing the workload.

Taking on too much

As discussed earlier, the problem of workload can also stem from an inability to say 'no' or poor delegation skills. Because we all tend to want to be liked by others, we often find it difficult to refuse requests because we fear our refusal may upset others or because we find it hard to say 'no' without feeling guilty. Our need to please others and the feelings of guilt and selfishness we experience when we assert our wishes are often a product of early childhood and cultural upbringing. Parents and teachers tend to reward the compliant rather than the challenging child. We soon learn that we are likely to be praised for doing what others want us to and punished for being strong-willed. This is particularly true for females, who are still generally socially conditioned to be acquiescent. Gender stereotyping remains pervasive in society, with different behavioural expectations for males and females; boys shout and act aggressively, while girls are expected and encouraged to be quiet, passive and co-operative.

Christian teaching carries many messages which encourage compliance and self-sacrifice. Examples include passages which declare that 'the meek shall inherit the earth' or which extol the virtue of putting up with an intolerable or unpleasant situation by turning the other cheek. These childhood and other cultural messages, particularly those which still reinforce the concept of social class, such as 'respecting one's betters', 'knowing one's place', etc., serve to reinforce attitudes of inferiority towards those with wealth, privilege, education and authority, and are very powerful in shaping adult behaviour.

Thomas Harris, in his book *I'm Okay – You're Okay: A Practical Guide to Transactional Analysis*, describes four fundamental life positions, as shown:

I'm okay You're okay	I'm not okay You're okay
I'm okay You're not okay	I'm not okay You're not okay

Adapted from Harris, 1969

1. I'm okay – You're okay. People who hold the 'I'm okay – You're okay' viewpoint see themselves as interdependent with others and their environment. Messages from others confirming that they are okay are appreciated and accepted, but are not essential to their feelings of self-worth. Such individuals feel confident and comfortable with who they are and what they are. They do not see themselves as being perfect, but as being okay. Because they realize that self-esteem is an individual responsibility they find it easy to see and respond to others as okay as well. If they have a problem, they will not hesitate to approach others and express it assertively. Because they see others as being okay, they expect that they will also be reasonable and responsive, and in conveying this attitude, people usually are!

2. I'm okay – You're not okay. People who hold this life position consider that the only person they can rely upon is themselves. In their viewpoint, other people are worthless and potential enemies, and their lives would be fine if other people would just leave them alone. Everything bad which happens to them is somebody else's fault. Anything good is all down to themselves. When they have problems at work, they are often unwilling to speak out, but inwardly fume and get angry or complain to others. They consider it pointless to speak out because they have already made up their minds that nothing will come of it. Alternatively, they bully, or act aggressively towards others.

3. I'm not okay – You're okay. People who hold the 'I'm not okay – You're okay' viewpoint believe that they are inferior to others. If they have problems at work, they tend to blame themselves because they are either incompetent or lack sufficient influence to be able to change things.

4. *I'm not okay – You're not okay.* People who hold this life position consider that they are worthless and so is everybody else. They feel disconnected from others and their environment, and have little motivation to try to overcome their negative feelings.

The concept of life positions is based on the theory that early in life, individuals adopt a fundamental belief about their own worth and that of others. According to Harris, this position may be determined as early as three years of age. Whilst the 'I'm okay – You're okay' life position is the healthiest, most individuals albeit unconsciously take up one of the other three positions. Harris argues that people only achieve the 'I'm okay – You're okay' approach by challenging their assumptions and consciously choosing to move to this life position.

The theory of life positions is worth considering seriously as it plays a major role in determining how we communicate and respond to others in our daily lives. Adopting the 'I'm okay – You're okay' life position is a fundamental precursor to assertive behaviour and effective delegation in the workplace.

Problems of work overload can be solved with good assertion and delegation skills. If an individual keeps on accepting more and more work, then one can be fairly certain that he will be given more and more work. If one individual is able to dump work on to others and they accept it without any objection, then that individual will be encouraged to repeat that behaviour. If your boss continually passes more and more of his workload on to you, this solves a problem for him. Most bosses tend to perceive their role as seeking solutions not looking for problems. If you are unwilling to speak out about the problem this may cause you, you can hardly expect your boss to necessarily recognize that there is one. It is important to tackle overload problems early before they escalate. People with too much work to do are more likely to make mistakes or miss deadlines. It is an unfortunate truth that whilst we are unlikely to get praised for the things we do, we are almost certainly bound to be reprimanded or remembered for the things we don't.

Some other ways of improving personal efficiency

- Some careful thought about the physical arrangement of your workspace can improve your efficiency and combat fatigue. A comfortable and supportive chair; an amusing and/or relaxing poster or print that you can look at to pick you up or escape to at difficult times during the day. If you are fortunate enough to be able to choose the decor of your work environment, select colours and furnishings with which you feel comfortable. When choosing colour schemes and furnishings for the home we all tend to consider such details to be important and take time making that choice. Yet many of us actually spend more time in our offices than we probably do in our sitting rooms at home.
- If you do a lot of writing and you are right-handed, then you should position your desk so that the source of daylight comes from the left.
- Working hard is not the same as working long hours. Creating 'sanity breaks' during the day, occasional changes of scenery (i.e. taking walks) and changing the layout of your workspace can be refreshing and stimulate creativity. Holidays are important; arrange your work around your holidays, not your holidays around your work. If you do the latter, then you are likely to find that you never have sufficient space in your diary to take any breaks. Book well in advance, pay for it and then go! Regular short weekend or midweek breaks can often be as refreshing as the more usual two-week periods, especially if you plan them for after busy work periods or outside traditional holiday times (i.e.

autumn, winter), when most people are in need of a pick-me-up.

- Invest in labour- and time-saving devices at home (e.g. dishwashers) to lessen your workload. Delegate jobs at home to others in the family and share the workload. Working women, because they often feel guilty about the time they spend outside the home, tend to overcompensate by continuing to do all the housework themselves. Perhaps because their own mothers were not in paid employment outside the home and so they lack any realistic and appropriate role model, many women often also feel guilty about employing outside help. They may even feel that paying others, usually other women, to do chores like the cleaning and ironing means they are in some way exploiting their own gender. Such feelings of guilt are misplaced and should be strongly fought and overcome. If you have one full-time and demanding job, then it is you who is being exploited, by yourself and by your family, if you take on another full-time job at home.

- Finally, remember the principle of creativity and the creative process. There are four stages in the creative cycle: Preparation (information collection), Incubation (idea generation), Illumination (solution recognition), and Verification (solution adaptation). Having collected information in the preparation stage, the next stage, the incubation of ideas, is critical. According to Graham Wallas (1926), an expert on creativity, incubation refers to the time in which the individual is not consciously thinking about the problem but nevertheless is making some progress towards its solution as ideas first encountered during preparation are maturing. The implications are that when faced with a complex or novel problem, impulsively seizing on the first solution that comes to mind may not necessarily be the best course of action. Allowing a period of incubation, putting aside the problem for an hour or two, perhaps sleeping on it, is likely to produce a better outcome. Whilst not still in conscious thought, the brain effectively never switches off but continues unconsciously to work on the problem comparatively free of conscious constraints. Nina Catterton of the University of Virginia has studied the physiological differences in the body's response when it is under stress as compared to in a state of deep relaxation. She has found that under circumstances of peak arousal the brain produces fewer creative beta waves, whereas when in a state of deep relaxation, more creative alpha or theta brain waves are produced. When people under immense pressure or stress report that they are 'just not able to think clearly', this is not exclusively a subjective expression of their current feelings but is the manifestation of a physiological change in body functioning.

Admitting inadequacies – being normal, not perfect

Nobody likes making mistakes or admitting that they can't cope, yet we all get things wrong or find ourselves in situations which we feel unable to resolve. Research has actually shown that although we tend to admire people who are capable and competent, we actually prefer people who, at the same time, we perceive also to be fallible. An American psychologist, Elliot Aronson, and his colleagues (1966) demonstrated this point by playing tape recordings of a programme called *Quizbowl* (the US equivalent of the British *University Challenge*) to a variety of people and asking them to rate how much they liked the contestants. The two superior contestants who answered 92% of the questions correctly were rated as more likeable than the average performers. However, of these two, the one who was unfortunate enough to spill his coffee during the show was the more liked. Another example of how human error, appearing less than perfect, may actually enhance others' opinion of us is cited by the evidence of researchers Rubin and McNeil (1983). In an opinion poll taken immediately after President Kennedy had approved the ill-fated Bay of Pigs invasion of

Cuba in 1961, the President's popularity was found to have actually increased as a result.

Seeking advice from others is not an admission of weakness, it is smart problem-solving behaviour. Most people, when asked for advice or help, are more likely to feel flattered and important rather than to view the suppliant as stupid or inadequate. Everyone likes to feel that they are regarded as some kind of expert in some field or other, particularly if the request for help or information is phrased in a way which makes them feel good, e.g. 'I feel that you are probably the best person to be able to help me, I'm having a problem with . . .' or 'I'm having a problem with X, I think I would benefit from your experience in this area . . .'

We all tend to be very good at seeing ways in which others could improve their performance or manage their lives better, but unless they ask us directly, we can be reluctant to offer that advice. Making a decision to ask advice of others can release a previously untapped source of information that can help us to manage a situation better – and we always have the alternative option of ignoring it!

Individuals often avoid admitting mistakes, not only because they are fearful that others will think less of them as a result, but because they wish to avoid criticism. Criticism can be extremely helpful provided that it focuses on facts, issues and behaviour and not personality, and gives some guidance and direction as to how the individual might do things better in the future. It is important when giving and receiving criticism not to become defensive or aggressive, as the situation will then easily escalate into conflict. If someone criticizes you, you ask them to specify exactly what it is about your performance that they consider needs improving and how you should go about improving it. Such a strategy will encourage helpful criticism and eradicate unhelpful or manipulative criticism.

Coping With New Technology

The movement towards the introduction of computers into the workplace to support and control information and mechanical systems had its beginnings in the early 1970s. Since then the growth in automation in the workplace, particularly the proliferation of visual display units (VDUs) and word processors (WPs), has steadily increased. According to the 1984 Industrial Relations Survey, during the period 1981 – 4 alone, 35% of office workplaces introduced computers or word processors which affected over a third of the workforce. Those most affected by the so-described 'technological revolutions' have been female workers involved in secretarial, clerical or administrative functions, predominately in the service sector.

Yet some twenty years on, despite this expansion in both commercial and domestic usage, the label 'new technology' is still applied to the phenomenon. This suggests that for the majority of individuals, working with computers is still perceived to be a novel, strange and consequently potentially stress-inducing experience. Indeed, the terms 'cyberphobia' and 'computerphobia' are now commonly used to describe the anxieties and stress-related reactions towards working with new technology. Computerphobia manifests itself in a variety of physiological, emotional and behavioural symptomology, including rapid heartbeat, nausea, diarrhoea, sweating and general feelings of panic and fear. This fear of computers relates not just to the anxiety and panic experienced by the individual when confronted with a computer screen or keyboard, but to a generalized negative disposition towards technology as reducing personal freedom and privacy, deskilling and depriving people of jobs. This fear and anxiety may also lead to avoidance behaviour (i.e. absenteeism or acts of sabotage).

The impact of new technology on jobs

Technological change involves much more than a change in the method of doing a job; it also represents a major social transformation in the workplace. For some workers – an estimated one quarter to a half of all knowledge-based workers by the year 2000 – it may even mean that the home becomes the workplace. The introduction of workplace

computers results in a change in the style of work organization; the physical layout of the office and a change in the
organizational culture. When computers are introduced, not
only does one have to acquire new operational skills, one
also effectively has to learn a new language. Whilst on the
one hand technology opens up opportunities for more flexible working arrangements, enabling people to work away
from a centralized workplace, it can also make work more
socially isolating, reducing social interaction and physically
restricting workplace movement. Technology often also
affects physical working conditions by increasing heat and
noise levels in the environment. It may also deprive the individual of the psychological need and satisfaction of physically handling things (such as documents, files, etc.), and the
tangible sense of achievement which comes at the end of a
productive day, when the earlier contents of an overflowing
in-tray have been transformed to a measurable pile of completed tasks in the out-tray. Furthermore, given the rapid
advances in technology, even relatively newly acquired
skills quickly become obsolete, and so typically it is not long
before the individual has to master new replacement
systems.

Research which has studied the impact of technology in
the workplace has found mixed evidence as to whether computers increase job interest and perceived skill utilization.
However, a number of studies suggest that computers are
perceived to increase workload and time pressure. Sonia Liff
(1990) recently conducted a study of over 200 female clerical workers in the West Midlands who had experienced
technological change, 48% of whom reported an increase in
workload. Nearly 40% also reported that office automation
had resulted in increased stress. Another study of VDU
operators in the insurance industry (Bradley, 1983) also
found that compared with non-users, computer users felt
more hurried and stressed, were more subject to frustration
at work and perceived their work pace as too high.

A major source of frustration amongst computer users is
system response time and breakdown. From the evidence of

Johannson and Aronsson (1984), there appears to be a generalized tendency amongst VDU operators to pace themselves at a higher rate in the mornings to guard against later breakdowns. Actual breakdowns, and also the expectancy of breakdowns, can become an appreciable mental strain, particularly for those users who deal directly with customer enquiries. Lack of control, amount of time spent at the terminal and feelings of constantly being watched or monitored, have been identified by other researchers as potential sources of strain and daily hassle. Monitoring systems have increasingly been developed which provide supervisors with performance indices such as the average number of key strokes per minute and the rate of production and error levels, and which serve to reinforce the operator's perception that Big Brother is watching.

Inadequate training and lack of consultation in system design and introduction appear to be common sources of frustration and stress amongst computer users. Although a UK Manpower Services Commission study in 1981 recommended that three months' familiarization was necessary before an experienced typist became a competent word processor user, in practice, the training users typically receive amounts to two or three days, plus on-site support. Overall, Liff concludes that whilst technology may change the nature of the job itself and increase task variety for some, it can also reinforce the current sexual division of labour in the office and reduce career advancement opportunities for women.

Health and safety issues

Over the years, computer usage has raised a wide range of health issues. Fears have been expressed as to the possible connection between VDUs and reproductive health, skin rashes, epilepsy, migraines, visual fatigue, musculoskeletal strain and potential radiation effects. Of the women who participated in Liff's study, three years ago, 63% reported experiencing increased eyestrain, 50% increased headaches, 43% more tiredness and depression and 28% increased backaches following the introduction of new technology. A number of studies have attempted to demonstrate a relationship between the time spent at the VDU and health effects. For example, Bradley's study found that those who used VDUs for more than two hours per day had more visual and muscular complaints than occasional or short-term users. Research which has examined the health aspects of new technology has in the main been inconclusive and is still continuing. One of the difficulties faced by researching this area is that of causal attribution. As the introduction of technology in the workplace results in a variety of independent yet related changes, it is hard to establish whether it is the technology itself or the stress and anxiety associated with these concomitant changes (e.g. the stress of learning a new job, increased noise, the repetitive and boring nature of the job itself) that is responsible for many of the adverse health effects experienced by users. As will be discussed in a later section, environmental factors such as lack of adequate air ventilation and poor air quality can present a hazard to health.

However, David Seddon of Coopers & Lybrand has drawn up some useful guidelines to help VDU users to overcome many of the common visual and postural problems associated with computer work.

- Generally speaking, epileptics should not be barred from using computer terminals. There is a risk that computers will aggravate an existing condition rather than cause epilepsy to develop in individuals with no prior history or pre-existing condition. However, people who suffer from photosensitive epilepsy may be susceptible to flickering lights and striped patterns. If you are epileptic, you have a 50% chance of a VDU initiating a seizure; it is therefore in your interests to inform your personnel manager if you do suffer from this condition.
- There have been a few reports of facial dermatitis, which appears to be linked to conditions of low humidity and very dry skin. Keeping the VDU screen clean with anti-static screen wipes is recommended to eliminate this risk.
- Stiff and aching muscles are often the result of spending

many hours locked in the same position. Also, certain muscles will become strained if forced or used to continually repeat tasks in the same way. Earlier in this section we suggested ways in which the postural problems associated with driving could be overcome by adjusting the seat position, ensuring that equipment is easily to hand and regularly and systematically relaxing the neck, shoulder, back and hands. Similar advice applies to computer users or anyone who spends long periods of time in sedentary work positions. Changing working habits, altering posture to ensure that the back is fully supported and the feet are flat on the floor, and moving about at regular intervals can prevent or minimize discomfort. It is recommended that a ten-minute break is taken for each hour worked at a VDU.

■ The ideal position when using a VDU is to have the angle of the body at around ninety degrees. The head should be aligned with the body and very slightly forward. Keep the elbows bent close to the body so that the forearms are at right angles to the body. Hands should be in a straight line with the forearms and wrists must not be allowed to droop..

■ Correct the position of the VDU to avoid reflections and glare. Regularly adjust the contrast and brightness of the screen to take account of light changes throughout the day. The top of the screen should remain at eye level or just below.

■ Sore eyes and visual fatigue can result from the movement of the eyes between the dark screen and bright surroundings and vice versa. Positioning the VDU at right angles to the window prevents light reflecting from the window on to the screen.

■ Have your eyes and eyesight tested regularly. People tend to blink less frequently when using the VDU. As blinking washes the eye, it is important to try to blink regularly, particularly if you wear contact lenses. Rest your eyes occasionally by looking off into the distance and use a document holder when copy typing.

In addition, it is important to maintain a flexible attitude towards technology; computers are here to stay and we all have to learn to live with them. Many of the problems inherent in computer usage stem from inadequate training and jargonistic and difficult-to-follow manuals. Unfortunately, one of the problems of computer manuals is that they are invariably written by computer experts rather than the average user. As you learn a system, keep notes as to how you accomplished the task and pass them on to other users. Better still, suggest to your organization that you and your colleagues prepare your own user-friendly guide to help overcome the problems that others might face in the future.

CHAPTER 3

Dealing with Difficult People at Work

The people we work with can be a great source of stress or create the environment and support to make life at work worth living. Our dealings with bosses, colleagues, customers, subordinates can dramatically affect our productivity and health, and indeed the way we feel at the end of each day. Hans Selye, the father of stress medicine, once said, 'Good relationships between members of a group are a key factor in individual and organizational health.' Even the prominent fiction writers of our time recognize the importance of relationships in the workplace. The main character in Joseph Heller's book, *Somethings Happened*, reflects on his relationship in an insurance company: 'In the office in which I work there are five people of whom I am afraid. Each of these five people is afraid of four people (excluding overlaps), for a total of twenty, and each of these twenty people is afraid of six people, making a total of one hundred and twenty people who are feared by at least one person.' He goes on in terms of his own department, 'There are six people who are afraid of me, and one small secretary who is afraid of all of us. I have one other person working for me who is not afraid of any, not even me, and I would fire him quickly, but I'm afraid of him.' Although humorously portrayed, many of the sentiments strike a psychological chord with many of us.

This chapter will explore difficult or problematic relationships at work and what can be done to cope with them. We examine the boss, colleagues, clients and customers and employee problems in general. We will start with probably the most significant and important relationship we have in the work setting, our boss.

Managing the Boss

We frequently read in management textbooks about the hows and whys of managing people, particularly subordinates or colleagues, at work. We rarely ever hear, however, about managing the most significant and central relationship we have in the workplace, the boss. Understanding how to manage bosses requires a special awareness of the different types of bosses, their personality needs, their management style and sanctioning behaviour, and, most important of all, the coping strategies that might be most successful in managing them. The purpose of this section is to highlight and explore the different species of bosses, in an effort to understand how best to deal with them in an organizational context. We will draw heavily on the work of Peter Makin, Cary L. Cooper and Charles Cox, in their book, *Managing People at Work*. We will highlight their various prototypes of bosses – The Bureaucrat, The Autocrat, The Wheeler-Dealer, The Reluctant Manager and The Open Manager – and discuss what they are like and how to cope with them. It is, of course, rarely the case that any particular boss fits just one of these types. If you want to be able to influence your own boss, however, you've got to know him and be prepared to take offensive or defensive action. Remember, as George Bernard Shaw wrote in *Mrs Warren's Profession*, 'People are always blaming their circumstances for what they are. I don't believe in circumstances. The people who get on in this world are the people who get up and look for the circumstances they want, and if they can't find them, make them.'

The bureaucrat

The bureaucrat is generally pleasant and mild-mannered, but is often excessively slow and cautious in making decisions. When faced with a problem or suggestion, his or her

66

usual response is to suggest that you check to see if the idea is in accordance with established custom and practice. If the problem or the suggested solution is novel, his or her response is to send memos to all those who are likely to be affected, asking for their reactions. According to Dean Acheson, the former US Secretary of Sate, the basic rule of a bureaucrat is that memos are sent not to inform the recipient, but to protect the sender. Subordinates would be well advised to read all memos when dealing with the bureaucrat.

In addition, a committee or working party might be formed to advise or decide on the issue. If you, as a subordinate, do anything in a way that is not sanctioned by the organizational rules and procedures, then you are likely to receive a reprimanding memo. This memo will be in addition to any possible verbal reprimand, and will be concerned with the way you went about the task, rather than about the outcome. Thus, you may actually be praised for what you accomplished, but admonished for breaking the rules to get the task done. These responses tend to have a demotivating effect upon subordinates, who tend not to bother taking any initiatives. If you want a quiet life, you learn how to work to the rules.

Personality needs. Like most managers, the bureaucrat is likely to have a high need for power. The main expression of this is in a need to control others, which can be achieved in a number of ways. According to Douglas McClelland, in his book, *The Achieving Society*, these range from sheer domination to subtle influencing techniques. Bureaucrats exercise control through strict administration of the rules. In this way, a high degree of certainty and predictability can be achieved. When their needs are blocked by higher authority, they tend to operate new instructions to the letter, waiting for a collapse so that they can say 'I told you so!'

Management style and sanctions. Bureaucrats will tend to be authoritarian, but will stay within the rules and their own limits of authority. They will tend to use the powers provided by the organization when dealing with subordinates.

These are generally those of *position power*, based on their position within the organization, and *resource power*, based on their control of rewards. When dealing with superiors they will generally be compliant but, if they believe that rules are being broken, they may use their control of information as a source of power. This may be used either positively, by the leaking of information damaging to a superior, or negatively, by holding back information that would allow the system to take corrective action.

How to cope. The best approach to deal with a bureaucrat type is to become fully familiar with the rules and regulations of your organization, so that you can present proposals in such a way that they are seen to be consistent with the system. If this is not possible, then avoid pushing your preferred, and possibly innovative, solution. Rather, present the problem, together with your own 'tentative thoughts' on the matter, as a request for help. Under these circumstances bureaucrats often show considerable ingenuity in redrafting your 'thoughts' so that they fit the current system, or in finding alternative interpretations of the rules.

The autocrat

Autocrats have very strong views on what ought to be done in any situation. These are derived from their own personal convictions concerning what should be done, rather than the organization's rules. They do not listen very well to their subordinates and issue instructions which they expect to be carried out without question. Such managers are intolerant of those who make mistakes and people who do not understand. They will get quite angry in these situations, but in a cold, withdrawn manner. Sometimes they appear inconsistent, since while they are autocratic with their subordinates, they are often helpful to their peers, and respectful in relations with someone higher up the organization. In the eyes of their subordinates, they can be either tyrants or benevolent autocrats, depending on their personal style.

Personality needs. Like the bureaucrat, the autocrat has a high need for power, but his source of power is his personal convictions, not the rules of the organization. There is research evidence to suggest that those with a high need for power are sensitive to power differentials, as Charles Cox and Cary L. Cooper highlight in their book on *High Fliers*. Their behaviour may vary, however, depending on whether the difference is in their favour or not. This would explain the apparent contradictions in their behaviour to different groups in the organization. If the balance is in their favour, as it is with subordinates, then direct power can be used. Faced with those who have greater power, they gain power by ingratiating themselves. This can be done by doing favours or flattering the more powerful individual. There is evidence to show that those managers with a high need for power do, in fact, respond positively to such ingratiation from their subordinates. With his peers, the autocratic manager can gain some temporary increase in his power by giving help when asked, especially if the other managers then feel in some way obligated.

Management style and sanctions. Like the bureaucrat, the autocrat will use those sanctions that his or her position in the organization provides. These are *position power* and *resource power*. If the organization accepts it they may also use *coercive power*. The benevolent autocrat is likely to use *resource power* quite effectively, giving infrequent, unpredictable, but large rewards.

How to cope. As with the bureaucrat, confrontation should be avoided unless on the basis of data. Because of the autocrat's need for power, the technique of ingratiation is often most effective. Again, because of his high need for power, he is sensitive to power from other sources. If the subordinate has more *expert power* than the boss, and is prepared to stand up to the autocrat, this may be respected. In general, if you have a source of power that is unavailable to your boss (normally 'expert' knowledge or information), then he or she will often cultivate the relationship. This is, however, a high-risk strategy, and should be tried with care.

The information or expertise you have may only be of temporary value. Sam Goldwyn, by all accounts an extreme autocrat, is reported as saying that he did not want to be surrounded by yes-men. He wanted everyone to tell him the truth, even if it cost them their jobs!

In extreme cases, autocrats are often brought down by a grouping of their subordinates. Realizing that their individual powers are not strong enough to confront the autocrat, political alliances are made between the subordinates, so as to increase their power base. An act by the autocrat that clearly and seriously breaks the organization's rules often acts as a trigger for concerted action by the subordinates. The autocrat is either removed or his or her powers strictly defined and limited, often by devolving power to a committee.

The wheeler-dealer
Wheeler-dealers are often very senior managers who spend much of their time negotiating with other departments over the allocations of resources and such matters as purchasing and sales. They clearly enjoy this type of activity and, as a result, spend a lot of time doing it, leaving their own department very much to run itself. They are not always successful in the negotiations, possibly because they are impatient and do not suffer fools gladly. When they are in their own department, they will make sorties around the staff, asking how they are getting on, checking on the progress of various projects. Staff are not given much guidance and are often left to sink or swim, but initiatives by staff are usually well supported. Non-performers tend to be ignored. There is a general feeling of dynamism in the department, but also a certain amount of chaos.

Personality needs. The wheeler-dealer is almost certainly an innovator type and if achieving the objectives means that the rules have to be ignored, so be it. We suspect that most are also high on achievement and are what is termed Type A

personalities i.e. hard driving, competitive, time-urgent individuals who tend to do everything in a hurry. Type A behaviour pattern is considered to be a significant factor in the
stress equation in that Type A's tend to have a heightened
perception of stress in the environment and are more vulnerable to its effects. Frequently, they are experienced by
others around them as 'stress carriers'. In contrast, at the
other end of the spectrum are what is termed as Type B's.
Type B behaviour pattern is characteristically relaxed and
calm. Wheeler-dealers are likely to have a high need for
power.

Management style and sanctions. The wheeler-dealer's
style may range from the consultative through the participative to *laissez-faire*. He often delegates quite considerably,
but sometimes, especially at times of stress, he may show a
flash of authoritarianism. Often he will regret this when
things cool down, and will smooth the feathers he has ruf-
fled. He often uses *personal power*, and people will work
hard for him because they admire him. Approval is withdrawn from those not performing up to the mark.

How to cope. With this type of boss, it is essential to
become proactive. Wheeler-dealers expect their staff to use
their own initiative and only value those who do. It is no use
waiting to be told what to do – nothing will happen and you
will be written off as ineffective. You should be prepared to
make your own decisions about what needs to be done and
then get on with it, making sure that the boss is kept informed. The boss should be informed rather than asked, the
assumption being that you will go ahead unless there are
objections. Keeping the boss informed also means that you
maintain a high profile with him or her. Problems with this
type of boss often centre on getting the more mundane jobs
done. The boss does not get pleasure from boring tasks and,
likewise, does not reward those who do them, no matter
how well. As a result, people learn that doing mundane jobs
does not pay off. Often they get thrust on to the most junior
member of staff (either in terms of seniority or tenure). If

you're in this position, you need to negotiate with colleagues to ensure that boring tasks are shared out evenly. Depending on your colleagues, it may be possible to do this by open agreement or it may be a more political process. Since the boss values enthusiasm and energy, find something to be enthusiastic about, hook his or her enthusiasm, then point out that mundane jobs are preventing you devoting your energies to it!

The reluctant manager

The reluctant manager will have been promoted on the grounds of technical competence. Reluctant managers generally leave their department to run itself, and they do not encourage their staff in any way. At the extreme, he or she could be described as someone who goes around stirring up apathy. If a technical problem arises then he will offer help, if asked, and this help will be highly effective. The management of the department, both internally and externally is ignored. In some circumstances, however, the reluctant manager may appear to be bureaucratic. Since he or she is not interested in managing, following the organization's rules provides the easy way out. When something non-routine happens, it is often very difficult to get a decision of any sort.

Personality needs. Reluctant managers are likely to have a high need for achievement, but a low need for power and affiliation. It is the low level of need for affiliation that is perhaps most noticeable. They are likely to be high innovators, but because they have no interest in management, this only shows in their technical activities. They are also likely to be Type B personalities, that is, not very hard-driving, time-conscious or people-sensitive.

Management style and sanctions. The management style of the reluctant manager is so *laissez-faire* as to be almost non-existent. Sanctions are rarely used, and when they are it is usually through the removal of social contact.

How to cope. The main problem with reluctant managers is getting them to engage in any interpersonal interactions at all. This, of course, has the advantage that you can get on and do whatever it is you like doing. Indeed, you could almost take over the running of the department yourself, if that is what you want. Because of their dislike of social interaction and management, any request for advice on managerial matters is dealt with in whichever way is quickest. This is in accordance with the principle that suggests that we spend longer on those jobs that we like. In these circumstances, it is perhaps best to use your control of information selectively. Present a number of alternatives from which the manager can choose, with your own preferred alternative strongly supported by evidence.

The open manager

This manager has a very firm belief in the value of participation and getting everyone involved. He or she holds regular meetings, *ad nauseam*, to review progress and decide on future actions, as well as *ad hoc* gatherings of subgroups or the department as a whole to deal with issues as they arise. Most people appreciate this, but there is the feeling that, on occasions, too much time is spent ensuring that all involved are committed when this commitment is not really necessary.

Personality needs. Open managers have little need for power, a high need for affiliation (supportive rather than assurance) and may have a high or low need for achievement. They are likely to be middle of the range between being an innovator or an adaptor in their approach to management issues. In addition, the open manager is usually flexible and in touch with his or her own behavioural needs.

Management style and sanctions. Such managers are highly participative and will only use *position* and *resource power* if and when required. They may also have some *personal power* and are admired by their subordinates.

How to cope. There are very few problems in dealing with the open manager, except perhaps in deciding how open you are going to be in return. The danger with being too open is that the information you divulge may be used to your disadvantage, either at another time, or by other people. A related problem may be that the manager is open in situations that may not be appropriate, for example, in relations with other departments who are behaving politically.

As the open manger engenders commitment, there is also a danger that you will become too involved and take more work on that is good for you. In these circumstances, you will need to say 'no'. Many subordinates may find this difficult, and learning to say 'no' in a positive way is a skill which has to be learnt.

Dealing With Colleagues

Relationships with our colleagues at work are critical not only to our productivity but also to our health and job satisfaction. Richard Lazarus (1966) of the University of California, Berkeley, has found in his research that supportive social relationships with colleagues at work are less likely to create interpersonal pressures, and will directly reduce levels of perceived job stress. Poor relationships between colleagues have been defined by University of Michigan researchers as 'those which include low trust, low supportiveness, and low interest in listening and trying to deal with problems that confront the organizational member' (Caplan et al., 1975). Indeed, their studies and others have concluded that mistrust between colleagues at work is related to high role ambiguity, poor communications and, very importantly, competition between colleagues (Cooper & Payne, 1988). As Bob Slocum in Heller's *Somethings Happened* illustrates, 'I always feel very secure and very superior when I'm sitting inside someone's office with the door closed and other people, perhaps Kagle, or Green or Brown, are doing

74

all the worrying on the outside about what's going on in the inside.'

Dealing with competitive and threatened colleagues

It is inevitable in organizations that there will be some element of competition between colleagues, in an effort to get promotion or to avoid redundancy or just to catch the eye of the boss. A certain degree of competition is healthy but it can also cause distress, particularly if it inhibits one's natural style of behaviour. The following case study, from a book by Murray Watts and Cary Cooper entitled *Relax*, illustrates the way in which colleague competition and an avoidance-coping strategy were counterproductive. Karen is a middle manager in a medium-sized company:

> Karen really wanted to do well at work but she realized that her male colleagues were threatened by her intellect. They were often sarcastic about her degree in business administration – 'Call yourself an administrator and you can't make coffee without spilling it in the saucer' – one joke after another. They liked it best when she was joking and laughing with them and playing the dumb blonde, and she was very good at that. So long as she played the part, she remained popular. But if she attracted the attention of her boss with the speed and quality of her work, then the mockery would start in earnest. So Karen chose to avoid being a success. But she became deeply resentful about playing the role that wasn't her. By avoiding success she kept the peace, but in 'keeping the peace' she lost her own peace of mind.

It should be obvious from this example that avoidance as a strategy of dealing with competitive colleagues can be personally damaging and increase anxiety levels. What is more productive is to recognize the signs that indicate that colleagues feel threatened, and then identify what may be the source of this threat. The signals that should alert you to threatened colleagues are as follows.

Signs of Threatened Colleagues

Covering up papers on his/her desk when you enter the room

Constantly opposing you at meetings when the boss is present

Hiding important files or materials from you

Undermining you with other colleagues and/or boss

Using memos as a means of conveying lack of trust in you

Noticeably excluding you from office/social functions

Animated conversations which turn to silence when you enter the room

---

Once you have identified that a colleague seems threatened or behaves in an excessively competitive manner, try and identify the reason. Is he or she threatened by your perceived competence, or your interest in a particular senior job (which he or she is also interested in), or by the boss's relationship with you, or is it some personality or management style incompatibility? Only by identifying the *source* of the problem can you begin to decide on an appropriate strategy to deal with it. Every strategy chosen has its pluses and minuses, the solution or coping strategy with the most benefits or pluses and the least costs or minuses is the one that should be pursued.

In addition, an appropriate response to threatened colleagues requires a positive attitude on your part, or what Jim and Jonathan Quick refer to in their book, *Organizational Stress and Preventive Management,* as 'constructive self talk' or 'positive mental monologue'. This monologue or self-talk can range from being gently positive or harshly condemning. When someone engages in 'negative self-talk', they achieve nothing and just maintain the stress, dissipating their emotional energy. If you are involved in constructive self-talk, it can achieve more positive task and psychological results. The following are examples of what the Quicks suggest in terms of being positive.

Constructive Self-Talk in Dealing with Difficult Colleagues at Work

Situation	Negative Mental Monologue	Constructive Self-Talk
Colleague hides important business file	'He's a nasty person, I'll just avoid him and hide material from his as well'	'I wonder why he is doing this, I will make an effort to get to know him'
Colleagues always puts you down at meetings, especially when the boss is present	'I'll fight him at every turn, preparing myself with more damaging material to undermine him'	'I let myself get disturbed too much by this colleague, maybe something's bothering him. I'll see if I can find out what it is'
Memos sent to other colleagues highlighting one of your business mistakes	'If that's the game he want to play, just watch my memos'	'Why did he need to send that memo? He must feel threatened by me. Have I done something to hurt him? How can I improve my relationship with him?'

In a sense, all these constructive self-talks are aimed at turning bad experiences into potential positive ones in our relationships with colleagues. It is all about thinking differently about stressful situations and therefore gaining some control. We don't have to be trapped into defensive or negative coping that can only make relationships and situations worse. We can make choices all the time. Murray Watts and Cary Cooper in *Relax*, provide an example of one's options in circumstances involving a colleague:

Supposing a workmate, who is known to fiddle the books and cheat his employers, is given promotion and you are passed over. Which reaction do you choose?

Headbanger
Furious anger at being treated this way. Take it out on others.

Pragmatist
Accept that this is an unjust fact of life. Get on with your work.

Reformer
Campaign for better decision-making in the firm, involving consultation at shop-floor level where there is better knowledge of the workforce. Discuss your concerns in confidence with respected peers.

Alchemist
Turn base metal into gold. Decide to turn this bad experience to good in any way possible. Equip yourself to cope when things don't go your way or even get worse. Make an informed decision to stay and be positive – or leave.

All of these reactions are possible options, or we might pass through them all in stages over a period of months – but to get stuck in the first option and never move on is a disastrous course of action.

Improving Customer/Client Relationships

As well as dealing with bosses and colleagues, many managers and staff in organizations have to cope with difficult or justifiably aggrieved customers and clients. As part of the Total Quality Management environment, many organizations recognize the importance of appropriately dealing with customers and clients. One large UK company has set the following quality standard procedure for dealing with customers complaints as part of their TQM programme:

If we all commit ourselves to quality and service there will be appreciably fewer occasions when our customers will need to complain, or indeed when we will need to complain to each other. But we do not live in a perfect world and occasionally we will be on the receiving end of complaints. At such times it will be important to:

- Apologize sincerely.
- See the complaint as a second chance to impress the customer. Good recovery when things go wrong can sometimes bring greater accolades than if nothing had gone wrong in the first place.
- Listen and do not argue. Recognize and appreciate how the customer feels.
- Collect all data and details so you can fully understand what went wrong.
- Accept responsibility, avoid passing the buck.
- Avoid excuses, they are unlikely to be appreciated.
- Find out what the customer wants; work out what you can do; and do it quickly.
- If there are things you can't do, say so and explain why not.
- Check that your action or promised action is acceptable to the customer and thank him or her for bringing the problem to your attention.
- Work out what you can learn from the experience and how you can stop it happening again.
- Contact the customer at a later date to ensure that there has been no recurrence.

This approach recognizes the importance of adequately dealing with difficult or unhappy customers, using a set of guidelines based on some basic psychological concepts. Other techniques might use Transactional Analysis (see Chapter 4) to understand where customers or clients are 'coming from'.

CHAPTER 4

Coping With Culture

So far we have dealt with the everyday hassles which occur in our immediate work environment. These are common sources of pressure and stress to most people in most work organizations. In this section, we will focus on the hassles that we are likely to encounter in a wider organizational context; hassles which are often more organizationally specific than those we have discussed already and are more a reflection of the particular culture operating in the organization. Situations like managing meetings, making presentations which we encounter when we leave the vicinity of our desk or immediate work group and its culture, and find ourselves having to function in a wider and often more uncertain work setting.

Coping With the Psychological Culture Of The Organization

Organizations, in functioning like mini societies, have distinct and identifiable cultures. Organizational culture is determined by a variety of factors including:

- History and ownership
- Size
- The technology employed and nature of the business
- The external environment and product market in which the organization operates
- Its people, particularly the organization's founders and leaders

Characteristically, organizational culture concerns symbols, values, ideologies and assumptions which operate, often in an unconscious way, to guide and fashion individual and business behaviour. In popular terms, it has been defined as simply 'the way in which things get done within the organization'. Organizational culture, like societal culture more generally, functions to create cohesiveness and maintain order and regularity in the lives of its members.

Different organizations within the same industry have different types of organizational culture. For example, the Grill Room at the Savoy and the local branch of McDonald's are both in the restaurant business, yet the experience of either working or eating as a customer at these establishments is qualitatively very different. An organization's culture is reflected in many ways, and influences not only its structure and managerial style but also the way in which it conducts its business in the widest sense. This includes the market strategy it adopts, the type and quality of customer service it offers, as well as creating a particular kind of psychological working environment for its employees.

When one joins a new organization, one has to learn the culture if one is to fit into the new work environment. This includes learning:

- The way in which people interact; appropriate terms of address, the organization jargon, acceptable forms of behaviour and dress
- the norms which govern the way in which work is organized and conducted, e.g. reporting arrangements, preference for written or verbal forms of communication
- the organization's self-image and the dominant values it espouses, e.g. the importance it places on particular organizational functions, the extent to which it wishes to be recognized as being tough or caring or environmentally friendly.
- what is expects of its employees and how it responds to its customers
- how the organizational game is played and the rules of

getting on in the organization, e.g. what it considers to be a good employee or an effective manager

According to American psychologist Roger Harrison, there are four main types of organizational culture: power, role, task/achievement and person/support (Harrison, 1972; 1987). In this section, we outline these different types and discuss how to recognize them in an effort to help the individual understand how best to deal with them.

Power cultures

The centralization of power is the most important feature of this type of culture. Characteristically, power rests with a single individual, usually the founder of a small nucleus of key individuals. Power cultures are generally typical of small organizations because they are often impossible to sustain as the organization grows larger, necessitating the diffusion of power, or as key individuals leave. Therefore, although more frequently encountered in small entrepreneurial organizations or traditional family businesses, certain large organizations which have continued to maintain a highly identifiable and often charismatic leader have managed to successfully retain a power culture. Because the emphasis is on individual rather than devolved group decision-making, power cultures have the advantage of being able to move and react swiftly, should they choose. Decisions tend to be based as much on intuition and past successes as on logical reasoning.

Long-established power cultures tend to be overladen with tradition. Offices and reception areas tend to display mementoes and pictures commemorating past achievements and former leaders. As they tend to retain a distinctly formal managerial style, outsiders frequently experience long-standing power cultures as being old-fashioned or conservative. The quality of service offered by power cultures is often tiered to reflect the status and prestige of the individual customer.

Power cultures can be further differentiated, in terms of

the type and perceived legitimacy of the power exercised, into the patriarchal as opposed to the purely autocratic.

The implications for the individual.   Whilst in power cultures individuals are frequently motivated out of fear of punishment, it is also important to recognize that in this type of culture, especially patriarchal power cultures, employee loyalty and long service is likely to be highly valued. Typically, rewards are given to the compliant rather than the challenging worker. Getting to the top frequently means maintaining visibility and ingratiating oneself with others in positions of power. It is important if one is ever to get to know what is going on in the organization to identify and cultivate a key informant within the power hierarchy.

To instigate any change, it is important not to debunk the past. The best chance of getting a suggestion accepted in a power culture is to present it as a natural and logical progression which builds on what has gone before. As power cultures are highly sensitive to criticism, it is preferable to present suggestions in a way which conveys respect for the past and ideally makes those in power feel as if it was their own idea. If you consider that you have been unfairly dealt with or have a worthwhile contribution to make, you may have to be prepared to go over your immediate boss and refer the matter to a higher authority; the closer to get to the top, the more chance you have of gaining a hearing. Power cultures may be difficult to change, but once they have made a decision to change, they respond quickly, so any new ideas are unlikely to get bogged down in red tape or committees. However, the best way to achieve change is undoubtedly to climb the greasy pole to the top and then change the entire culture – provided you have the stamina and willpower to do so.

Role cultures
The role culture epitomizes the Weberian concept of a bureaucracy, its guiding principles being logic, rationality

and the achievement of maximum efficiency. The organization's view of itself is as a collection of roles to be undertaken rather than a collection of people/personalities. This culture is frequently encountered in large organizations, with highly specialized divisions of labour. Because commercial organizations with role cultures tend to be exclusively results-oriented, finance and accounting are often recognized as being the most important functions.

In a role culture, things get done according to the corporate bible – usually in triplicate. Consequently, formal procedures, role requirements, authority boundaries and regulations concerning the way in which work is to be conducted are central features of this type of culture. Power tends to be hierarchical and comes with the job description. Role cultures tend to be extremely status-conscious and often breed competition between departments or divisions, particularly when budgets are discussed. One gets to know how important an executive is in the organization by the size of his or her expense account, the amount of budgetary discretion he or she can exercise, the type of car he or she drives and the quality of the furnishings of his or her office. Organizations which depend upon mass volume sales and standardized product quality, such as McDonald's, reflect the scripted type of customer service associated with role cultures.

The implications for the individual. Role cultures function well in stable conditions, but their high degree of formalization, numerous committees, etc. makes them slow to change. In the past, therefore, they offered the individual a high degree of security and a clear sequential career path. However, whilst they are predictable and reasonably fair environments to work in, they are frequently experienced as impersonal and often frustrating.

In role cultures, it is important to recognize that a good employee is one who recognizes protocol and always sticks to the rules. Your competency will be judged above all else by your ability to fill in the right forms, get the right signatures and submit them before the prescribed cut-off date.

Provided you recognize the bureaucratic priorities, master the systems and can quote the rules, nothing too dreadful will happen to you. Expertly learning the way round the systems will earn you the respect of your boss and your colleagues. Provided you can suggest ways in which new ideas can be incorporated within the system, they will be well received. Because role cultures nurture meetings like horticulturists nurture plants, the ability to manage meetings and make effective presentations is extremely important in both getting on and introducing change into role cultures.

Task/achievement cultures
The salient features of task culture are the emphasis it places on accomplishing the task, and the energy it directs towards securing the necessary task-related resources and skills. Task cultures tend to exist *within* organizations (e.g. in specific departments such as Research and Development) rather than *as* organizations, although the culture is often found in new start-up organizations, particularly in new technology. A task culture is a team culture, in that commitment to the specific task bonds and energizes the individuals. It is the specificity of the task requirements rather than individuals or formal rules and regulations which dictates the way in which work is organized – *what* is achieved is more important than *how* it is achieved. Consequently, relevant expertise is highly valued and often more important than personal or positional power.

Task cultures are characterized by their flexibility and lack of formal authority. They seek to offer their customers tailored products which meet their individual needs.

The implications for the individual. Task cultures tend to encourage creativity and autonomy, and are often highly satisfying cultures in which to work. However, they do make high demands on the individual and can be exhausting and turbulent environments in which to work. To survive in a task culture, it is important to be able to handle conflict effectively and be prepared to criticize and take criticism constructively, for when things go wrong, everybody tends to blame everybody else. Burn-out is an inherent problem of task cultures, therefore it is important that an individual working in this type of culture recognizes the dangers and strives to maintain an equitable balance between work and leisure.

Person/support cultures

The main characteristic of the person/support culture is egalitarianism. In person/support cultures, structure is minimal; the culture exists and functions solely to nurture the personal growth and development of its individual members. Information, influence and decision-making are shared collectively. The organization is subordinate to the individual for its existence. Not surprisingly, in its purest form, it is more often found operating in communities or co-operatives (e.g. the kibbutz) than in profit-making enterprises. It may also be encountered in certain professional partnerships (e.g. doctors, dentists, barristers' chambers), where there is a common agreement to share facilities such as office space and secretarial services.

The implications for the individual. Despite their emphasis on collectivism, person/support cultures can be rather isolating environments to work in because of the emphasis that is placed on leaving the individual to do his own thing. Individuals within person/support cultures are encouraged to take responsibility for their own self-development; it is therefore the type of environment in which independent and highly self-motivated individuals are likely to do well.

Once the individual has recognized and learnt the culture of the organization, he or she can adapt to work *with* rather than *against* the grain of that culture and so avoid unnecessary distress. However, individuals who find themselves working in an organizational culture where there is a total mismatch between individual/organizational values and preferred style of working, are likely to develop long-term stress (see Chapter 5).

Managing Meetings

Attending meetings has become a key feature of organizational life. It is estimated that managers in large organizations typically spend 22% of their time at their desks and a massive 69% of their time in meetings. The overt purpose of any meeting is to make decisions and circulate information. Psychologists have long argued that group decision-making results in greater acceptance and commitment to the decision. However, whilst this may be the case if the meeting is well managed and the group genuinely work together and reach true consensus, many meetings are time-wasting, unproductive and result in conflict and ill-feeling amongst members.

There are three levels to any group discussion:

1. the meeting has an explicit task or agenda
2. it has established conventions governing the way in which social interaction between members is expected to be conducted through the operation of everyday courtesies
3. there is a more covert emotional level at which feelings such as fear, insecurity and aggression make themselves felt. Consequently many meetings have what is termed a 'hidden agenda'

It is at this third level that many of the problems associated with meetings arise. Hours can be devoted to elaborate game-playing between members, or discussion of a wide variety of red herrings which detract from the original purpose of the meeting. Game-playing occurs with such frequency that one suspects that for many people the true purpose of any meeting is exactly that – to play games and make mischief. Meetings, therefore, become an exercise in role-playing. The most common roles played in meetings are (Cooper, 1991):

The chairman

The most formal role is that of chairman. He (and it is usually a he) is in a position to set the agenda and a good chairman will keep the meeting running on time and to the point. Sadly, chairing a meeting well is an art which many chairmen lack. This is often because they are ill-prepared and unassertive, and allow certain individuals to dominate the proceedings or digress from the agenda. Consequently, rather than controlling the meeting, they allow other informal role-players to gain the upper hand and control them.

The constant talker

Chief of these role-players is the constant talker, who just loves to hear the sound of his or her voice. It is often a man, whose criterion of success is the percentage of the total conversation he can dominate. Sometimes the constant talker also combines this role with that of the self-appointed comedian. The self-appointed comedian is unable to distinguish between informal and flippant behaviour. Consequently, he constantly throws in humorous comments and may even embark on an epic funny story which bores everyone for hours. The constant talker only attends meetings to speak, rarely to listen, and whilst he may have experience of everything, he is often the expert on nothing.

The anal-retentive type

Another key role is what Freud would have called the anal-retentive type. Often a prolific note-taker, he or she insists on clear definitions and constantly seeks clarification, tending to refer back to earlier points throughout the discussion. The anal-retentive is the 'dot the i and cross the t' type of person who bores everybody present with his or her pedantic attention to detail – with the exception of fellow anal-retentives, who admire his or her thoroughness.

The 'can't do' type

Then there are the 'can't do' types, the people who always find reasons why something can't be done, usually based on some minor technical problem. This is the person who will point out, for example, that you can't have the Annual General Meeting on that day because they happen to know that some other (usually insignificant) meeting is taking place on the same day.

The 'can't do' types are cunning, wanting to maintain the status quo. Since they have often been in the organization for a long time, they frequently quote historical experience as a ploy to block change: 'It won't work, we tried that in 1964 and it was a disaster.' When they are not challenging others with the 'it won't work' dialogue, they sit silently, eyebrows raised, shaking their heads.

A more subtle version of the 'can't do' type, the 'yes, but . . .' , has emerged recently. He or she has learnt about the need to sound positive, but still can't bear to have things changed.

The red-herring type

These are the people who love meetings and want them to continue until 5.30 p.m. or beyond. Irrelevant issues are their speciality. They are also relatively cunning and *need* to call or attend meetings either to avoid work or to justify their lack of performance or simply because they do not have enough to do.

The counterdependent

The red-herring lovers are joined by the counterdependents, those who usually disagree with everything, that is, particularly if it comes from the chairman or through consensus from the group. These people need to fight authority in whatever form, but are usually so obvious in their disruptive behaviour that a smart chairman or group can easily marginalize them.

Other roles played at meetings are 'the regular attender', 'the social worker' (who resolves emotional conflicts between group members), 'the whispering smartass', the non-participating cynic', 'the fence-sitter' and, of course, 'the silent type'. The latter is present in all groups and most other members project on to him lofty motives or objectives, such as 'he is above this juvenile exercise; or 'he will only speak if he has something significant to say'. Usually, the silent type is just shy, insecure and plain bored.

There are also common ploys or games that are played at meetings:

'Hey, look at me!'

An individual ploy is attracting attention. Meetings give ambitious combatants an arena in which to compete in front of the boss, a kind of civilized forum in which corporate gladiators can perform before the organizational princes and emperors. Meetings can also provide attenders with a sense of identification of their status and power. In this case, managers arrange meetings as a means of communicating to others the boundaries of their exclusive club; who is 'in' and who is not.

Mark McCormack, of International Management Group, got so fed up with staff wanting to be included in meetings that he set up a formal company-wide one. Its purpose was not to discuss company business, but simply to make everyone feel good because they were all invited. Everyone got the point.

'I thought of it first!'

A popular game is pinching someone else's suggestion. This is where someone, usually junior or female, makes an interesting suggestion early in the meeting which is not picked up. Much later, the game is played, usually by some other more senior figure who propounds the idea as his own. The suggestion is of course identified with the player rather than the initiator.

'You can play Mum!'

Another increasingly common game, as more women enter the world of work, is casting the woman in the role of secretary or Mum. The game is usually initiated by someone who is threatened by an overzealous or extremely competent female colleague. The purpose of this game is to de-professionalize the woman by forcing her into a traditional role of

minute-taker or coffee-dispenser or sending her out of the
meeting to copy any documents which may be required. By
inveigling the female colleague to appear in a less serious or
professional role, the player feels less challenged by her.

'Shopping a colleague'

Another game is SAC – shopping a colleague. This game
takes many different forms, such as to point out that a particular individual's contribution is irrelevant, because that
subject was discussed at the previous meeting at which he or
she was not present, or to exclude from the agenda someone's particular achievements. Alternatively, it may involve
subtly letting it be known in a meeting that X was not at an
important meeting or conference, or implying that the
player has a particularly close and confidential relationship
with the individual's boss, so that whenever the individual
makes a suggestion, the player puts down by saying 'That
won't wash with the director, I *know* he was very much
against the idea when we spoke recently.' The list of SAC
game plans is endless.

'Well, I think that about covers it?'

Because so many meetings end in confusion and without a
decision, another more communal game is played at the end
of the meeting, called 'reaching a false consensus'. It couches
its so-called decision in such a vague way that a number of
interpretations are possible. Everyone is happy, having
spent their time productively. The reality is that the decision
is so ambiguous that it is never acted upon, or, if it is, there is
continuing internecine conflict, for which another meeting is
necessary, to the absolute delight of the red-herring types
and the regular attenders.

In summary, for many, meetings provide the opportunity for
social intercourse, to engage in battle in front of the boss, to
avoid unpleasant or unsatisfying work and to highlight social
status and identity. It would seem that they are, in fact, a
necessary though not necessarily productive psychological

sideshow. But what then can be done to make meetings more productive? Apart from recognizing the roles and games that are being played and taking steps to minimize the disruption they may cause, the following tips are also useful.

Tips for a better meeting

■ First of all, before you call a meeting, consider whether the meeting is really necessary. How long should it be? Who should be there? When and where should it be held? Many people become regular attenders at meetings because they were invited once as a guest to one specific meeting, were noted in the minutes and then automatically were included on every subsequent circulation list. Check with people in advance whether they consider their attendance is absolutely necessary before sending out invitations. People often feel obliged to attend meetings because they are invited, not because they really want to or feel they should be there. More often than not, they would be just as happy receiving a brief summary of the discussion.

■ Aim to limit the size of the meeting to no more than seven, whenever possible. The larger the group, the less time-efficient the meeting becomes. Increased size also has the effect of reducing commitment.

■ An effective chairperson is critical, one who is sufficiently assertive to interrupt wafflers and allocate time limits to discussion. Directing discussion through the chair may be rather formal but it curtails interruptions and affords everybody the opportunity to have their say. If the official chair is ineffective and starts to lose control, someone else needs to unofficially and tactfully take up the role.

■ Record actioned minutes with the name and initials of the person required to take action alongside. This ensures that everybody receives clear and specific instructions as to what they are required to do.

■ Use 'brainstorming' techniques to generate ideas, either within the meeting time or by asking individuals to brainstorm their ideas, but not censor them, in advance of the meeting.

■ Makes notes on flip charts or whiteboards of points that the meeting may need to come back to later; this way good suggestions will not get lost as discussion continues.

■ Suspend all telephone calls and ban portable telephones from any meeting.

■ Regularly change the seating arrangements and the meeting place, to break up cliques and to avoid set patterns of interaction and thinking. Most people, given the choice, are likely to take up a position opposite their boss and next to a close colleague.

■ Remember meetings are about listening as well as talking. To win a hearing at a meeting, it is important to listen actively to what others say. When making your point, demonstrate that you have heard what has been said, by acknowledging what has gone before, and show that you understand that it is important, then raise your issue. Avoid jumping in and putting other people down, try to build on their ideas. Convince others of your point by focusing on the facts and issues, rather than attacking personalities. Otherwise they are likely to retaliate by personally attacking you and the situation will escalate into conflict.

Making Presentations

'It's not just a matter of life and death; it's much more important than that!'
(quotation attributed to former Liverpool FC manager, Bill Shankley, prior to an important game)

If there is any single event in organizational life which is guaranteed to make most managers break out into a cold sweat, it is the prospect of having to make a presentation. Managerial jobs place a high emphasis on verbal communication skills and so managers are frequently asked to present findings or make a case orally to their board or colleagues, to speak to the press or address various interest groups outside the organization. Furthermore, the ability to deliver a good oral presentation is increasingly becoming an accepted and important feature of many selection and assessment procedures within large organizations.

Presentations have several advantages over written reports. The more important ones being that:

1. they are more personal and more imperative
2. they are less easily ignored
3. any misunderstandings are more immediately evident and can be re-explained or expanded upon
4. feedback is more immediate

Unfortunately, however, a bad presentation is better remembered than a badly written report.

People are generally fearful of presentations. Performing in public is an area of human activity for which most people traditionally receive little or no formal training. Throughout our school and university education, success is essentially evaluated on the ability to pass written rather than oral examinations. Consequently, getting up and speaking to large groups of people is perceived to be an alien and potentially uncomfortable experience and one most of us often do our utmost to avoid.

Most of the fear and stress associated with making a presentation arises from the speculative 'what if' scenarios which run through an individual's mind, for example 'What if nobody laughs at my jokes?', 'What if I dry up?', 'What if somebody asks me a question I can't answer?' In the same way that actors talk of 'dying' on stage, the aspiring manager dreads that a bad presentation may amount to career suicide.

Reducing the area of the unknown

Anybody who regularly watches *News at Ten* will be familiar with the standardized format which it follows each evening. Firstly, the programme begins with a series of brief headlines which alert the viewer to the issues/news which are to be discussed. These issues are then addressed in more detail. Finally, the programme closes with a further short review of the main points. Furthermore, the viewing audience know in advance that the entire news presentation will be over within thirty minutes, which is ideal in terms of the length of the average viewer's concentration span. The format of *News at Ten* illustrates what are recognized to be the three fundamental structural principles of any presentation:

1. Tell them what you are going to say! (The Opening or Exposition)
2. Tell them! (The Main Body – the Development of Ideas)
3. And then tell them again! (The Closing Recapitulation)

The key to any good presentation is preparation. The more that the presenter can reduce the area of the unknown, the more confident and in control he or she will feel. Many of the things that go wrong with presentations and throw the presenter off balance – for example, arriving at the venue anticipating an audience of around a dozen, only to find an expectant audience of close to one hundred sitting there – can be avoided with some basic research and advance planning. Preparation begins with five important questions:

WHY are you giving this presentation? Is it to give information, obtain a consensus, initiate a course of action or entertain? At the end of the presentation, what do you hope to have achieved?
TO WHOM is it addressed? Who will be in the audience? How much do they know already about the subject? What do they expect to learn? What questions or objections are

they likely to raise? Approximately, how many will be there?

WHERE will the presentation take place? What will the layout of the room be like? What audio-visual equipment will be available? What do you need? Will a microphone be necessary?

WHAT are you going to say? Make a list of all your points.

HOW will you make the presentation? and how long will you be expected to talk?

The what and the how

Before making a presentation, you have to plan carefully what you are going to say and then rehearse and time it. First impressions are very important, so every presentation needs a good opening to build the confidence not only of the speaker but also of the audience, so that they can sit back and relax, reassured that they are in capable hands. A good opening does not necessarily have to include a joke, although it can help. If you are not confident that you are a good or a natural joke-teller, avoid jokes altogether – when they go flat, they can be extremely embarrassing.

However, before you even start, check first that everybody can hear you and will be able to see any overheads or slides you may use. Having to repeat yourself in a louder voice after a false start can seriously undermine confidence. Begin with a few welcoming courtesies, introduce yourself and state what you are going to present. It is important to outline your route map. Remember that your audience do not know what you are going to say. This means fortunately that they won't know what you miss or might forget to say. However, people listen better when they are prepared for what's coming next. To avoid the possibility of them switching off in the first few minutes, give them a few signposts by briefly explaining the structure of your presentation, including how long it will last and when they can ask questions. Most presenters feel more comfortable handling questions at the end rather than dealing with them as they go along. This allows them more control over the proceedings. They are also less likely to become sidetracked and lose concentration if the flow of the presentation is uninterrupted. Also, the odds are that many early queries are likely to be automatically covered during the course of the presentation.

It has been suggested that most business presentations can be structured using a 6P plan:

PREFACE (Introduction)
POSITION (Current situation)
PROBLEM (What it is)
POSSIBILITIES (Alternatives)
PROPOSAL (Suggested or recommended solution)
POSTSCRIPT (Outcome/presentation objectives)

As you move from one part of the presentation to the next, you will need to introduce a paragraph to enable the audience to make the connection. Otherwise you may lose them. Psychological research has shown that people remember material better when it is presented to them in categories or headings. In presentations, these labels have to be given verbally and/or presented on overheads or slides.

In 1972, Bransford and Johnson conducted an interesting psychological experiment which illustrates the importance of triggers such as headings in switching on attention and aiding memory recall. They presented subjects with the following information and then asked them what it was about.

The procedure is actually quite simple. First, you arrange items into different groups. Of course, one pile may be sufficient depending on how much there is to do. If you have to go somewhere else due to lack of facilities, that is the next step; otherwise, you are pretty well set. It is important not to overdo things. In the short run this may not seem important but complications can easily arise. A mistake can be expensive as well. At first the whole procedure will seem complicated. Soon, however, it will become just another facet of life. It is difficult to foresee any end to the necessity for this task in the immediate future, but then one can never tell. After the procedure is complete one arranges the materials into their appropriate places. Eventually, they will be used once more and the whole cycle will then have to be repeated. However, that is part of life.

Until they gave the subjects the simple heading 'Washing Clothes', the piece was virtually unintelligible; many people had switched off after the first couple of sentences.

Finally, close with a brief summary, a word of thanks, take a deep breath and invite your audience to ask questions.

Some helpful hints on content and style

- Avoid jargon and acronyms. They may be unfamiliar to your audience; even if they are members of your own organization.
- Have some form of *aide-mémoire*. Numbered postcards with your key points on are excellent. They can be easily and unobtrusively held in your hand. It is a good idea to note on these cards the point at which you wish to introduce a slide or overhead and to write in cues for yourself like 'smile' or 'pause'.
- Pauses are important. When a person is nervous or excited, he or she tends to speak faster than normal; this is particularly true of females who normally speak faster than males anyway. Deliberately taking time to pause helps slow down delivery, can help emphasize or punctuate what you say, and gives you a chance to take a deep breath.
- If you are using autocue you will need to prepare a script of exactly what you are going to say and adhere rigidly to it, otherwise the autocue operator will become confused – and subsequently so will you!
- Remember when you are preparing that written language can sound strange when spoken. Use short

punchy sentences and words you would use in normal conversation.

- If you are quoting statistics, rather than giving exact numbers, which take time for the memory to process (e.g. 1,627), round them up or down and quote approximately (e.g. approximately 1,600).
- Try to include hypothetical examples or analogies to illustrate what you are saying.
- Remember the concentration span of your listeners. In any listening situation, there is always a strong primacy-recency effect. The listener is more likely to recall what you said first and last, and probably only about 50% of what you said in the middle. Ideally presentations should be no more than 45 minutes including questions.
- If your presentation is intended to be persuasive and re-sult in a commitment which involves financial expendi-ture, sell your idea first, then present the costs at the end.

Visual aids

Any presentation is usually more effective if it appeals to more than one sense in terms of interest and reinforcement of the verbal message. Typically, this is achieved by visual aids (i.e. overhead transparencies or slides, or handouts). However, if it is appropriate to the presentation, passing around work samples (e.g. machine parts) to illustrate what you are taking about can be extremely effective, in that they appeal to two senses simultaneously, (i.e. sight and touch).

When preparing visual aids, it is important not to include too much; three or four brief points in large typeset are suffi-cient. Detailed financial information or complex flow charts are better presented in the form of individual handouts which people can study whilst you talk. Be careful if you ex-periment with colour; colour transparencies may look pretty, but some colours, such as blue, are extremely diffi-cult to read at a distance. It is good practice to use a pointer

in order to avoid the common mistake made by many presenters of standing silhouetted by the screen and masking
the actual transparencies. Arrange your slides or transparencies in order before you start. Try not to include too
many; their purpose is to aid your presentation not turn it
into a picture show (a video would do the job much better).
About five or six transparencies are generally sufficient for
an average-length presentation.

A whiteboard or flip chart can be good for impromptu
illustrations but lengthy use interrupts the flow as your back
is to the audience. Slides tend to be more expensive than
overhead transparencies. Also, their ordering is particularly
crucial as they have the problem that it is more difficult to
flip back or flip on if you need to refer back or are running
out of time. Asking a colleague to take responsibility for
operating the slide projector can relieve stress and leave you
free to concentrate on what you are saying, provided they
are adequately rehearsed. Sometimes, the siting of the
speaker's platform in relation to the projection equipment
necessitates the use of an extra hand.

Some basic do's

- Rehearse – ideally rehearse in front of others and ask
  for feedback. Alternatively, practise in front of the
  mirror, or videotape or record yourself. Critically listen
  to yourself; remove and replace words which you find
  yourself stumbling over. Watch out for the overuse of
  catch phrases such as 'if you know what I mean', and
  annoying physical mannerisms such as fidgeting. If you
  are involved in a group presentation, practise as a
  group, and familiarize yourself with what others are
  going to say in order to avoid overlap and to ensure that
  if a member suddenly goes sick or gets delayed in
  traffic, you can act as understudy.
- Never read verbatim from notes, nor try to memorize
  the whole presentation. If you are reading, you cannot

maintain eye contact. If you look up and you are dependent on a verbatim script for what comes next, the chances are when you look down that you will have lost your place and will panic! As everybody who has ever sat an examination knows, memory can also be very unreliable under conditions of extreme stress.

■ The practice of placing a sheet of paper over an overhead transparency and gradually sliding it down to reveal each individual point fortunately is no longer fashionable. The benefits to be gained by doing this are generally overshadowed by the irritation it causes the audience.

■ Distribute any handouts at the end or as you go along; never in advance. If you do this, people will read the handout rather than listening to you. You may also be inadvertently setting yourself up for some tricky questions at the end.

■ Remember eye contact is important. If you panic, find a friendly face in the audience and fix on it. Smiling from time to time is also important.

■ Finally, seek the honest feedback of someone you know in the audience so that you can learn from the experience and improve next time.

Handling questions

The key to handling questions well is not to get defensive and possibly end up arguing with the questioner. It is a good idea to ask from the outset for questioners to identify themselves prior to putting their question. This will give you a handle on what their interests or motives are in raising the question, so that you can appropriately tailor your answer. In a large audience, it is also appropriate to ask questioners to stand up to deliver their question so that you can hear it clearly. If you don't fully hear a question, do not attempt to answer the bits you have heard and guess at the rest; ask them to repeat the question.

Repeating the question back to the questioner is a tactic

used by many experienced presenters, particularly politicians. It has a twofold purpose. It ensures that the rest of the audience hear the question clearly, and gives you a few seconds breathing space to work on your answer. If you do not know the answer to a question, do not bluff; the questioner may be smarter than you and by bluffing he or she may expose you for what you are. The way round such a question is firstly to try to make the questioner feel good; he or she has raised an interesting and complex question – it must be or you would already have thought of it – so acknowledge it. Then either throw the question open to the floor, or admit that it is something you haven't thought of in any depth, but would like to discuss in some detail with the questioner, perhaps after the presentation?

Managing stress

We have discussed in some detail ways and techniques for preparing and delivering effective presentations. In this section, we provide a few final tips for calming pre-presentation nerves:

- Arrive head of time so you can check out the room one final time and compose yourself.
- Avoid eating or drinking in the hour before, for obvious reasons. When under stress, digestion slows down and the urge to urinate increases and so can make for an uncomfortable presentation. Many actors suck a boiled sweet before a performance to moisten the mouth and combat dryness. Blackcurrant lozenges are reported to be particularly effective.
- Check yourself out in a mirror before you go on. The unzipped fly (or, in the case of females, the ladder in the stocking) may be a music hall joke but you don't want it happening to you.
- Practise deep breathing and a few relaxation exercises to release tension.
- Voice delivery and projection is better if you stand up to present.

- Have water, no ice (you may inadvertently choke on it), at your side and when you pause take a sip to keep your mouth moist.
- Practise, practise, practise . . .

Talking to the press

Working as a senior manager in either the public or private sector nowadays means dealing with the press. Environmental concerns, redundancies, mergers and acquisitions, and joint ventures are only a few of the issues that increasingly force contact between managers and the media. The skills of dealing appropriately with the media, whether newspapers, TV or radio, are not usually found on MBA courses or indeed in generic management training courses. In order for managers to reduce the hassles or stress associated with press coverage of corporate events, it is important to remember some simple rules:

1. Prior to a press conference or media interview write down the two or three points you would like conveyed.
2. Remember, for press and media interviews 'bad news is good news', so be careful and stick to your planned points – don't deviate.
3. Don't appear defensive, keep your points short and wait for the next question. Try not to fill in silences; wait to be asked the next question rather than rambling on, otherwise you might say something you will later regret.
4. If you don't have an immediate answer, indicate that you will get back to your questioner on that point, asking him to call you later that day or the next.
5. If you are called up and asked for an immediate response to some important corporate problem, don't respond until you have thought through the implications of your alternative responses. Ask the questioner to call you back later in the day.
6. If you can turn a negative event into a positive one,

highlighting some future action in the same or allied area, do so. On the other hand, if the event or incident is patently your organization's fault, and if legal advice permits, own up to it and describe future action to rectify or prevent such events from occurring again.

Organizations should be cognizant of the importance of external communications, not only in terms of their image but also in minimizing the potential stress for the manager confronted by the media. Regular courses on interviewing skills should be conducted so that managers are better able to deal with these events as and when they occur.

Living in the Physical Environment

The quality of the physical working environment is recognized as an important factor in employee health and safety. Factors such as noise, lighting, smells, temperature – particularly extremes of temperature – poor ventilation and over-crowded offices can affect our moods and overall mental state. Bad housekeeping practices, old or poorly serviced machinery and equipment, inadequate safety apparel and lack of training can lead to unsafe behaviour and accidents in the workplace. According to research, where the workplace is relatively hazardous, new recruits and employees returning after a period of absence are particularly vulnerable to suffer a workplace accident.

In 1983 the World Health Organization defined the concept of 'sick building syndrome'. Sick building syndrome is characterized by a range of physiological symptoms including sensory irritation, headache, nausea, dizziness and fatigue. Characteristically, these symptoms grow worse over the course of the day and disappear after the workers leave the building. Scandinavian research by Peder Skov, Ole Valbjorn & Bo Pedersen (1989) has found the concentration of macromolecular organic dust, floor coverings, the number of workplaces in an office, the age of the building and other indoor climatic factors to be associated with the occurrence of the syndrome. As discussed (in Chapter 2; Coping with New Technology), the introduction of new technology (i.e. VDUs and word processors) may exacerbate the problem of poor ventilation. However, the Scandinavian research has found that mucosal irritation, sinus problems, etc. are also associated with psychosocial and job-related factors such as dissatisfaction with one's supervisor and work overload. The same study also found that office workers who considered their work pace too fast and felt that they had little influence over their work activities were significantly more likely to report general symptoms. Again, these factors have been shown to be specific sources of stress amongst computer operators (these are discussed in more detail in Chapter 2).

In the light of continuing health and safety legislation and EC directives, physical working conditions are becoming a high priority amongst responsible employers. The recent successful case brought by Veronica Bland against Stockport Metropolitan Borough Council for compensation in respect of bronchial-related problems attributed to the workplace smoking of colleagues has further highlighted the issue. However, if it is to be improved, health and safety must become the responsibility of everybody in the organization. It is therefore important that every workplace accident, regardless of whether it results in any personal injury or not, is reported, as well as any near misses or potentially dangerous practices or incidents. Any suggestions for the improvement of the physical working environment should be made direct to the individual's manager, designated health and safety officer or union official. Finally, spending all day in the same room in a relatively sedentary position, irrespective of the quality of the physical environment, is likely to cause an individual mental and physical fatigue. It is therefore important to discipline oneself to take adequate breaks, stretch one's legs, and get some fresh air.

Improving Communication Within The Work Environment

'"When I use a word" Humpty Dumpty said in rather
a scornful tone, "it means just what I choose it to mean
– neither more nor less."'
(Lewis Carroll, *Alice in Wonderland*)

Poor communication, or even lack of communication, whether at work or at home, can be both an important source and a manifestation or consequence of stress. As will be discussed in more detail in the next chapter, one of the major sources of stress amongst acquired or merged employees was found to be lack of communication. Similarly, when employees are experiencing high stress levels, there is a tendency to withdraw and communicate less or to distort communication.

The effectiveness of organizational communication can only be realistically measured in terms of relative dissatisfaction, given that it is an area of organizational activity which has to constantly strive for improvement. Nobody is ever totally or consistently happy with the amount, frequency or level of information they receive, even those at the most senior level in the organization.

Communication is a vast subject which can never be adequately covered in a volume as slim as this. Throughout the book, virtually every hassle we have or will discuss touches on the issue of communication. However, in this short section, we have chosen to focus on one particular theory of communication, transactional analysis (TA), which we consider to be useful in improving interpersonal communication in the workplace. In outlining the theory and its implications, we will draw heavily on the work of Mary and Charles Cox.

Transactional analysis.

The theory of transactional analysis was originally developed by Eric Berne in 1961, and is a set of concepts which provides a comprehensive and useful way of analysing the way

106

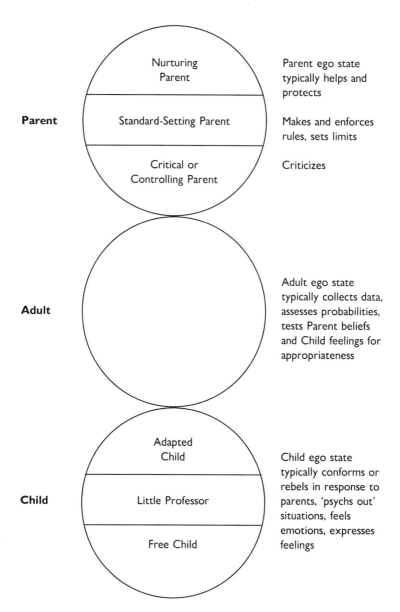

Personality structure: the three ego states
Source: Cox & Cox 1980

in which people relate and interact with each other. In TA terms, these interactions are termed 'transactions'.

According to TA theory, each individual possesses three 'ego states'. An ego state is a consistent pattern of feelings and experiences which gives rise to a corresponding pattern of behaviour. The three ego states are:

The Parent ego state is a storehouse of significant others' attitudes, feelings and ways of behaving. It provides us with our values, opinions, social consciences, rules and regulations. The Parent has three main functions – the active giving of care and support (the Nurturing Parent), the caring use of prohibition to protect and sustain (the Critical or Controlling Parent) and the provision of limits and standards (the Standard-Setting Parent). A person acting from the Parent ego state is behaving according to their system of values.

The Adult ego state is the unemotional, rational ego state. It is the part of the person which collects and processes information and events in an objective way, weighs alternatives, tests reality and makes decisions based on present and past experience. When a person acts from the Adult ego state, they operate free of strong feelings.

The Child ego state is a collection of childhood experiences, feelings, reactions and decisions. It is the energy source and the source of natural emotions and behaviour. There are three kinds of child behaviour – spontaneous, natural responses (the Free Child), responses which are determined by social pressure and norms (The Adapted Child) and intuitive, problem-solving behaviour (the Little Professor). A person whose strong feelings are triggered is operating from the Child ego state.

The Transaction

A transaction is a unit of social interaction; a series of transactions forms a conversation. During a transaction, a message originates in one person's ego state and is sent to a

particular state of another person. If the other person responds from the ego state addressed (i.e. there is a parallel
or complementary transaction), then communication between the two parties will be experienced as satisfactory and
the conversation may continue indefinitely.

Example of a parallel transaction Adult to Adult

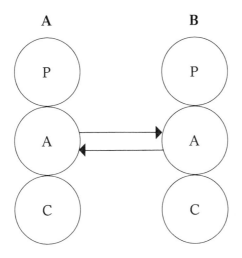

A   'What time is the meeting?'

B   'Four o'clock.'

Example of a complementary transaction Nurturing Parent to Child

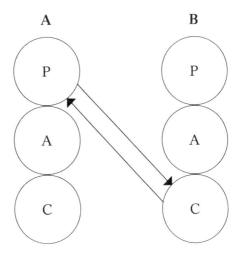

A   'You look worried. Do you need some help?'
(Parent to Child)

B   'Yes, please, I don't know how to structure this report.'
(Child to Parent)

Example of a complementary transaction Critical Parent to Child

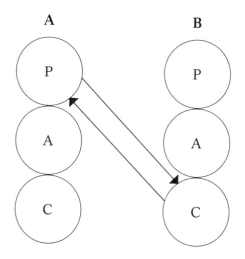

A   'You've got these files in a right mess. Sort them out.'
        (Parent to Child)

B   'Yes, I'll do it right away.'
        (Child to Parent)

Problems occur in transactions when a person receives a response from an ego state other than the one addressed. This is termed a 'crossed transaction'. The effect is to stop the dialogue, even though this may be only momentarily. The other person may then have to readjust and move from one ego state to another in order to satisfactorily continue the dialogue. If they don't, the communication will be experienced as unsatisfactory and may develop into conflict.

Example of a crossed transaction

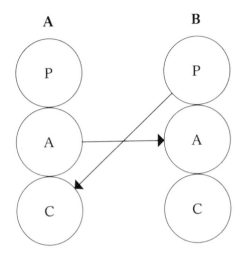

A 'Where are the latest sales figures?'
(Adult to Adult)

B 'I don't know, you're always losing things.'
(Critical Parent to Child)

Sometimes there are 'ulterior transactions'. According to Mary and Charles Cox (1980), 'These occur when there is an overt courteous "social" transaction (what is seen and heard out aloud) and at the same time a covert "psychological" transaction which may or may not be experienced consciously by the person involved.' If there is an ulterior transaction, attention will be paid to the covert level, whether this is in awareness or not. It is not uncommon for people to report after a conversation that they were vaguely aware that 'something else was going on'.

Example of an ulterior transaction

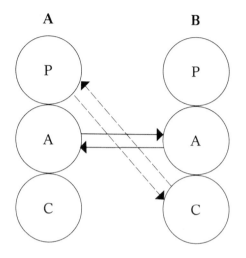

A	'Do you have a lot on this morning?'	(Overt level;
B	'I'll have to check with my secretary and let you know.'	Adult to adult)
A	'I have to see you about that accounts fiasco.'	(Covert level;
B	'Not today you won't!'	Parent to Child, Child to Parent)

   Transactional analysis provides a useful way of analysing interactions between organizational members. For example, most criticism is usually directed from Critical or Controlling Parent and expects a reply from Adapted Child. In other words, the critic expects the person receiving the criticism to passively accept it and respond contritely. In reality, what usually happens is that the person being criticized either responds rebelliously from Free Child or retaliates from Critical or Controlling Parent. Consequently, the criticism becomes destructive or is ignored. The criticism is likely to be constructive if the transaction is parallel, from Adult to Adult, as it will be unemotionally focused on specific acts, issues and behaviours rather than on personalities.

CHAPTER 5

Unexpected Workplace Events

In earlier chapters, we have focused on potentially stressful events and situations which are a relatively common feature of everyday working life (e.g. travel, work overload, poor organizational communications, etc). In contrast, this chapter considers the extraordinary and unexpected workplace events which develop rapidly and are difficult to foresee, but which are perceived to be of major consequential importance. Dealing with travel stress may require the individual to modify his lifestyle or replan his work schedule, but it is unlikely to cause him to rethink totally his entire career future, as may the experience of sexual harassment or company takeover.

Stress is commonly experienced as resulting from a situation or event in which the individual perceives himself to have little or no control over what is happening. Typically, the individual feels that he is being overtaken by events which he has no effective strategy for dealing with. If that situation or event is totally unanticipated, increasingly the individual will come to see himself as an innocent victim of it with the subsequent stressful effects and consequences inevitable and beyond his control. Congestion at peak travel times on the M25 may be stressful but it is also predictable. If an event is predictable, the individual can be prepared for it and take steps to avoid or minimize its negative effects. However, in contrast, for the vast majority of employees involved, the sudden announcement of a company merger or takeover bid constitutes a destabilizing and potentially stressful event which could not be anticipated or predicted and for which they are totally unprepared. Consequently, in such circumstances, the sense of helplessness and injustice experienced by the individual is heightened. The unanticipated and untimely nature of such events often fuels considerable anger, bitterness and frustration. Characteristically, this invokes the response 'Why did this have to happen to me *now*, at a time when everything seemed to be going so well?' or, alternatively, 'at the time when I have more than enough on my plate as it is?'

This is often because such events are both *novel* as well as unexpected and so, therefore, are considerably removed from the normal realm of everyday experience. In other words, there are no past solutions from any remotely similar life experiences to draw upon which would seem to suggest ways in which the individual might satisfactorily regain control of the situation. Obvious examples of such events occur in the course of one's personal life (e.g. an unplanned pregnancy, the discovery of a partner's infidelity or the unexpected death of a close family member). As has been mentioned, coping with mergers and acquisitions or sexual harassment are examples of workplace events which fall into a similar category. Redundancy and ethical dilemmas are also unexpected and potentially distressing workplace events. Whilst the published divorce rates and unemployment statistics may indicate that many others are going through the same experiences, this often provides cold comfort to the individual who finds himself in this situation.

Coping With Mergers and Acquisitions

During the last ten years, merger and acquisition activity has continued at an unprecedented level, both in the UK and overseas. In the 1980s, over 7,000 stocklisted companies were acquired within the UK alone. At the same time, many others became party to join venture agreements and other forms of strategic alliance, which resulted in substantially changed terms of ownership. Many of these mergers and joint ventures occurred in traditional industries such as brewing, engineering and manufacturing, as well as the service sector, which has experienced considerable market consolidation in the same period. This trend towards partnering for competitiveness has increasingly involved foreign investment in UK companies (e.g. the Fijutsu takeover of ICL, the GEC-Alsthom engineering merger). The last decade also saw many state-owned industries become privatized, a trend which seems set to continue. Such events, in that they have resulted in major organizational restructuring and changes in working practices and procedures, have had a major impact on the day-to-day working lives of thousands of employees.

Merger and acquisition activity may be increasing in frequency, but for those affected it is still an extraordinary and destabilizing life event, generating enormous uncertainty and requiring considerable personal adjustment. The magnitude of that adjustment and its associated stress has been universally rated as being equivalent to the gain of a new family member or becoming bankrupt, and more stressful than events such as mortgage foreclosure or the death of a close friend (Holmes & Rahe, 1967). Indeed, the American psychologist, Professor Philip Mirvis, has likened the psychological response to a merger to that of personal bereavement. Another researcher, David Schweiger (Schweiger, Ivancevich & Power, 1987), has related the emotionality of the event to the sense of detachment a young child experiences if separated from its mother.

According to Mirvis (1985) one can expect that employee reactions to a merger will pass through the four stages commonly associated with personal loss:

Stage I: Disbelief and denial
Typically, the individual's first reaction is extreme shock. He/she may deny that the acquisition or merger will ever happen despite circulating rumours or a bid announcement. Even when the deal is actually signed, the individual may strive to convince himself that nothing will change. Frequently, an existing organizational leader is identified as a

champion of the status quo, who will successfully fight to preserve the established identity and culture of the organization and will not abandon, compromise or sell out the company.

Stage II: anger through rage and resentment

As the reality of the situation becomes more obvious, feelings of shock and disbelief are replaced by anger and resentment towards those considered responsible. This anger may be directed towards the old management, the new merger partner, the state of the economy, the government, or even the world in general.

Stage III: emotional bargaining, beginning in anger and ending in depression

As fear and uncertainty about individual job future develops, this anger often turns inward. The individual becomes angry with himself for not anticipating the event. He may come to resent the commitment and loyalty he has invested in the company. Often, the individual becomes increasingly nostalgic for what is past. Feelings of anger may subsequently subside to be replaced by depression.

Stage IV: acceptance

Finally, the individual comes to recognize that what is past is gone forever, and accepts that he must face up to the new situation.

Until there is acceptance that any attempt to deny or resist the situation is futile and unproductive, a positive approach will not begin to develop. Fixation at Stages I, II or III will result in preoccupation, unproductive behaviour and negative feelings, and is likely to be experienced as stressful. It may cause the individual to become withdrawn or perhaps to leave the organization. Similarly, even if the individual comes to accept the situation, he or she may still feel let down by the old organization and no longer be as committed to or satisfied with their work or the organization. As well as dealing with the sense of loss and discontinuity at the passing of the organization, the individual also invariably has to cope with the uncertainty associated with major organizational change and with the concomitant stress.

The psychological impact on the individual of merger and acquisition and its implications for individual and organizational outcomes was the subject of a large-scale research study recently conducted by the authors of this book (Cartwright & Cooper, 1992). This research examined the experiences over time of a number of mergers, acquisitions and joint ventures between organizations involved in the same area of business activity which resulted in the large-scale integration of two previously separate and discrete workforces. They ranged in size from small ventures, where there were fewer than 100 employees, to a large UK and a pan-European merger which involved several thousand employees. During the course of this research, interview and questionnaire data was collected from over 750 individuals affected by merger and acquisition activity. This research is still continuing and the size of the database has now increased to over 1,000 employees. Measures were taken to assess levels of organizational commitment, job satisfaction and mental health at various points in time during the merger/acquisition process.

The model of occupational stress presented in Chapter 1 conceptualizes potential sources of stress in the workplace as emanating from six general areas of work-related behaviour and experience. Any major organizational change, such as a merger or acquisition, is likely to impact on all of these areas, possibly simultaneously. Therefore, it is not surprising that the study concluded that mergers and acquisitions are particularly stressful because they are perceived as being an important event in an employee's working life over which he or she has no control, precipitating change for which the individual has not self-selected and is psychologically unprepared. The number and range of potential merger stressors is extensive. Whilst not intended to be an exhaustive list, the most common stressors are:

- Loss of identity/increased organizational size
- Lack of information/poor or inconsistent communication
- Fear of job loss/demotion
- Possibility of job transfer/relocation
- Loss of, or reduced power, status and prestige
- Disturbed or uncertain career path
- Changes in rules, regulations, procedural and reporting arrangements
- Changes in colleagues, bosses and subordinates
- Ambiguous reporting systems, roles and procedures
- Redundancy and devaluation of old skills and expertise
- Personality/culture clashes
- Increased workload

According to Professor Jack Ivancevich (Ivancevich, Schweiger & Power, 1987), on the announcement of a merger or acquisition, the individual makes a cognitive appraisal of the situation to determine the extent to which the event is likely to affect them personally. This appraisal may take any of the forms below.

Perceptions of the individual of the merger situation	Resultant outcome
As having no effect on the individual	An irrelevant appraisal
As a challenging opportunity for the individual	A positive appraisal
As having harmed or damaged the individual in some way (e.g. reduced self-esteem or conferred a sense of powerlessness)	A negative appraisal
As potentially threatening to the individual	A negative appraisal

Because organizational communication during a merger

or acquisition is characteristically poor, and there is also a considerable time lag between bid announcement and the introduction of any actual changes, individuals respond to their perceptions as to the *likely* changes which may result. Almost universally, these perceptions are typically pessimistic, and collective uncertainty manifests itself in a widespread 'fear the worst' syndrome. Consequently, negative appraisals tend to dominate.

Whilst the prospect of being taken over as opposed to merging ostensibly would seem to be potentially the more traumatic experience, on the basis of their research Sue Cartwright and Cary Cooper (1992) concluded that in reality, the reverse was the case. Mergers, as they create greater and more prolonged uncertainty, were found to be more stressful and have a longer-term adverse effect on mental health than acquisitions. In support, the authors provided evidence based on a survey of over 150 senior and middle managers involved in a large UK merger in the financial services sector. Despite the lack of hostility and high degree of cultural compatibility between the merger partners, mental health measures taken approximately six months post-merger showed that over a third of the managers surveyed had mental health scores comparable or higher than psychoneurotic outpatients. Furthermore, the findings indicated that the merger had been significantly more stressful for managers of the numerically smaller merger partner.

Mergers differ from acquisitions in a variety of ways which would seem to make them inherently more stressful for those involved. Compared with acquisitions, mergers result in the following:

1. substantially more role duplication or overlap which is likely to promote competition and jealously as organizational members jockey for position
2. the power and resultant culture dynamics of the combination are more ambiguous. Considerable uncertainty and speculation frequently surrounds the issue as to who is calling the tune

3. perhaps, more importantly, because the time between the announcement and the introduction of any actual change is generally much longer with mergers than acquisitions – a year or more is not unusual – they result in unacceptably long periods of organizational limbo. Consequently, individuals feel less inclined to commit themselves to any future plans they might have had which involve any major financial expenditure or personal investment (i.e. holidays, home improvements, further education, etc.), and resort to living their lives on hold

Whilst the accommodation of change is often stressful, the uncertainty of anticipated change and the duration and intensity of that uncertainty has been shown to be more stressful for most people than the change itself (Cartwright & Cooper, 1992). This conclusion has been further supported by subsequent research into the effects of privatization on public utility employees (Nelson & Cooper, 1993).

What can the individual do?
Because of the financial importance of mergers and acquisitions, a considerable amount of managerial time and energy is expended in negotiating and completing the deal itself. Typically, merger and acquisition negotiations and discussions tend to centre almost exclusively around financial, legal and strategic considerations, at the expense of people issues, which are generally forgotten or ignored.

It has been suggested (Searby, 1969) that so much energy is frequently expended at the negotiation stage that the acquiring management is often too exhausted and apathetic to manage the merger effectively. Certainly, the evidence would suggest that the absence of any well-conceived human integration plan or management strategy for dealing with people, coupled with a lack of sensitivity, is a common feature of most merger and acquisition situations. There are a variety of ways in which mergers and acquisitions could be managed more effectively to alleviate or reduce their stressful effects on the individuals involved. These might include:

- more information and earlier involvement of the human resource function pre-merger, perhaps through the conduct of some form of human merger audit
- more joint consultation and opportunity for employee participation
- organizational recognition that mergers are stressful, perhaps through the provision of stress management courses/counselling services
- the provision of merger telephone hot lines or people specifically appointed to confidentially and sensitively handle any post-merger grievances or anxieties
- the establishment of objective and fair merger reselection procedures

Whilst there are many initiatives which the organization could introduce to help reduce merger distress, the individual with no previous experience of this kind of situation is likely to consider his or her options to be extremely limited and so feels obliged to passively wait and see what happens. Prima facie, the only possible action that could be taken by the individual to regain control would seem to be to seek alternative employment and physically remove himself from a stressful situation.

There is considerable evidence that many employees do decide to take this course of action. Research studies published in the mid 1980s (Unger, 1986; Walsh, 1988) report levels of voluntary resignation amongst senior executives as high as 25% to 50% in the first year post-merger. Abnormally high rates of labour turnover following mergers and acquisitions are not exclusively confined to senior managers and occur at all levels of the organization. Cartwright and Cooper (1992) found that the overall rate of staff turnover across all levels of employees, even during a period of economic recession, in certain circumstances can be as high as 60%. However, resignation may not necessarily be a sensible or practical course of action, especially if motivated by anger or outrage. This is particularly the case for older or long-serving employees who may risk losing potentially substantial redundancy payments or jeopardize or disrupt their pension arrangements.

Breaking out of the 'fear the worst' syndrome

Universally, the most stressful aspects of merger and acquisition are fear of job loss and living with uncertainty. Fearing for his own survival, characteristically the individual is likely to be reluctant to admit to others in the workplace, particularly superiors, the degree of stress he is experiencing, as this may jeopardize his job future by indicating that he is not 'merger fit'. Consequently, most merger stress remains covert and bottled up during worktime and is only let out or discussed at home with close friends and colleagues.

Of the individuals surveyed post-merger by Cartwright and Cooper, 78% considered that the merger had to some degree caused them stress. 20% reported that they had coped badly and had not developed any effective strategy for dealing with the situation. Approximately 25% reported that the main strategy they had used to combat stress was by talking with their spouse or partner. Whilst the social support of family and friends is an important and useful strategy for coping with stress, because the consequences of major organizational change may have important family repercussions (e.g. job loss or relocation), endlessly speculative discussions around the dinner table about the plethora of nightmare scenarios which might happen only serve to heighten anxiety at home. Talking about the situation may make the individual directly affected feel better, but in doing so, it may effectively transfer that stress to his or her partner, as the following scenario illustrates:

Typical scenario

John Jones, a 37-year-old regional sales manager, is married with a dependent wife, Ann, two young pre-school children and a large mortgage. His company have announced that they are to merge with a considerably larger operation. John feels his position is particularly vulnerable because of the overlap in sales territories. This fear is shared by his sales team. Rumours are already circulating that his patch will soon come under the hammer. He is aware that his most successful sales representative has already been approached by a competitor.

Because John is concerned that if the performance of his team starts to slide, this will affect the outcome of any carve-up of his territory, he is anxious to maintain morale and keep the team motivated. Consequently, at work he tends to play down the situation and tries to convey a business-as-usual attitude and so not disclose his own anxieties.

Once at home, these anxieties surface. Ann has always been interested and supportive towards his career, and so each evening he discusses his merger-related worries with her. His wife listens sympathetically but feels totally impotent in alleviating his fears. Searching for reassurance and advice, she takes to discussing John's situation with her friends and neighbours. This only serves to increase her anxieties. Whilst friends empathize, it seems that everybody she speaks to has a bad luck or merger horror story to tell of unfairly and insensitively displaced executives.

Ann becomes increasingly angry and irritated with John for burdening her with the anxieties of a problem she feels powerless to resolve, for his obsession with the merger and his resultant lack of interest in her life. She finds herself unable to switch off to the situation and continue with her day-to-day activities. She finds herself snappy with the children. She also comes to dread John's return from work to relate the latest rumour or counter-rumour. Her attitude becomes less sympathetic and she is no longer prepared to listen to John's endless monologues, and so acts to avoid any discussion of the subject. John becomes upset by his wife's apparent uncaring and unsupportive attitude; relationships at home deteriorate and he starts to regularly call in at the pub on the way home.

Outcome. Originally, John had problems at work; he now also has problems at home. The one strategy he had for dealing with a distressing situation, externalizing his worries by talking to Ann, is no longer available to him. Drinking may temporarily obliterate the negative mental dialogues and inner turmoil he is battling with, but is is more likely to exacerbate his problem rather than solve it. In the long term, his work performance and psychological health are likely to be adversely affected, so increasing the likelihood that he will lose his job.

Alternative. Many of the problems associated with mergers and acquisitions stem from lack of official communication and information, and fear of the unknown. This void in communication is then automatically filled by rumour and scaremongering. In a merger situation, the rumours which travel the furthest and the fastest are invariably of a negative nature. There is seldom anything more pervasive than collective misery. In drawing parallels with other merger experiences, stories of merger casualties are more likely to be remembered than those of successful merger survivors. Because rumours are verbally communicated, they are particularly vulnerable to distortion and exaggeration, as anybody who has ever played the game of Chinese Whispers will recognize. Attending to rumours is a mentally tortuous and unproductive activity.

Rather than confronting the rumours with his superior, John responded by sharing his fears exclusively with his spouse. Whilst there are benefits to be gained from openly discussing anxieties with others, John unfortunately went into overkill and so effectively destroyed the support that Ann was originally prepared to offer. Ann's support may have helped John vent his feelings and possibly put the situation into a more rational perspective, but she was not in a position to dispel the veracity of the rumours or reassure John that his job future was secure. Hence her increasing feelings of powerlessness.

John may feel it helpful and necessary to talk things over

with Ann. However, he would have found her support more likely to continue if there had been some prior negotiation and acceptance of Ann's position, on John's part, by:

1. agreeing to restrict discussion of his merger problems to a mutually agreed and ruthlessly enforced pre-set time limit (e.g. perhaps setting aside a half-hour each workday evening to discuss the topic), rather than letting it dominate their entire conversation
2. acknowledging to Ann that he accepts that the purpose of these discussions is primarily to help him express his feelings and that he does not expect Ann to come up with any solutions
3. building on his strong family relationships rather than wearing them down, by planning and becoming more involved in family activities and making the merger subject totally taboo at the weekend
4. working towards a more positive and informed evaluation of the situation

Avoiding negative mental monologues: seeking alternative constructions

As discussed, the way in which an individual perceives an event or situation dramatically affects the stress response experienced. The announcement of a merger or takeover represents a crisis or critical point in an individual's working life. Certainly, it is a time to take stock and to reassess achievements to date, in both the work and the personal domain. The Japanese word for 'crisis' means both 'a threat' and 'an opportunity'. However, typically in such circumstances it is the perception of threat and fear of the worst which makes the event so stressful. To be able to deal with merger stress more effectively, the individual needs to be able to reverse the characteristically negative mental monologues of self-talk which achieve nothing and maintain stress, and focus on the more constructive and equally positive ways of viewing the situation. Thought-stopping, or the ability to recognize non-constructive thoughts, attitudes and behaviours and stopping them immediately, is a very effective strategy for coping with stress. One extremely influential senior executive of long standing is reported to have a sign in the hallway of his home directly opposite the front door which reads 'NOW STOP THINKING ABOUT WORK!!' This sign is apparently an extremely effective trigger for him to put aside the problems of the day, which in any event he can probably do nothing about until the morning.

In a merger situation, it is important for the individual not only to recognize and stop non-constructive thoughts and attitudes, but also to be able to replace them with more constructive self-talk alternatives, for example:

Typical mental monologue. 'Oh God, I shall lose my job.'

Alternative construction. 'I might not necessary lose my job, but if it should happen, is that really the worst thing that could happen to me? I will still have things that I value more (e.g. good health, family, etc.). Was I really that happy with the job I was doing? If I was to be made redundant, are there alternative jobs/goals that I might be able to pursue but which my present situation prevents me from doing?'

Personal stock-taking. Conduct a personal stock-take. List down on paper the following:

	In the work domain	**In the personal domain**
Your personal strengths and weaknesses	....	....
Your skills and talents	....	....
Your achievements	....	....
The times and occasions when you		

	Work-related	Non-work-related
really felt good about yourself	....	....
Past opportunities which you regret not taking	....	....
What you have to offer the organization	....	....
What the organization has to offer you	....	....
Your short-term goals (for the next six months)	....	....
Your mid-term goals (for the next five years)	....	....
Your long-term goals (five years and beyond)	....	....
The short-, mid- and long-term goals of other members of your family	....	....
Your financial assets and liabilities	....	....
Your monthly expenses (i.e. first-priority expenses)	....	....

Formally conducting this kind of exercise serves several useful purposes:

- it can put the work situation into perspective.
- It can help identify or stimulate ideas of possible alternative job/career options.

129

- Prior analysis of personal strengths and achievements in terms of what the individual has to offer this or any subsequent organization can be beneficial in positively enhancing self-concept and serve as helpful preparation for any subsequent merger reselection interview.
- It directs the individual towards non-work-related and family goals. Work-related goals may be temporarily on hold at this point in time, but there are likely to be other non-work-related goals which the individual could focus upon and move towards during this period of uncertainty, many of which (e.g. learning a foreign language, improving inter-personal skills, etc.) may necessitate an investment in time rather than any substantial financial commitment. As well as providing a useful diversionary activity, this would also help the individual a regain a sense of control over an aspect of his life, and combat the numbness and behavioural inertia often associated with the merger event. Focusing on goals which involve skills development is likely to improve psychological health and may also possibly enhance future career prospects.
- Reviewing one's financial situation at the outset may help the individual pinpoint areas of unnecessary expenditure where cutbacks could be made in the future – should the worst happen.

Completing this activity at this time is likely to be valuable in helping the individual more positively focus on the future rather than dwelling in the past, and so move to a state of psychological acceptance of the situation. However, life-planning reviews should not be conducted exclusively in response to a crisis but rather become an exercise that the individual undertakes on a regular basis. Many life goals are not achieved overnight but require systematic planning, otherwise they never move beyond the realms of wishful thinking. Recent research (Holmes & Cartwright, 1993) has found that whilst many individuals desire to change their career in mid-life, those who successfully achieve a career change are more likely to have researched and planned their career move a long time in advance.

Typical mental monologue. 'Things will never be the same again; the culture will change and everything will be different. Past experience and loyalty count for nothing. There'll be a new man at the top with new ideas who will bring in all his own people. It'll be a case of change, change, change . . . and more change, and all for the worse!'

Alternative construction. 'Sure there will be change; it might be for the worse, but equally things might get better. This organization is not perfect and certainly could be improved. If I give it a fair chance, once I get used to it, I might prefer working in the new merged organization. The increased organizational size, combined strengths and stronger market position might actually improve my future job security and create more opportunities not fewer.'

Organizational stock-taking. A great deal of merger stress is created by fear of the unknown. David Altendorf (1986) in his study of the Getty-Texaco combination concluded that the first thing organizational members do in a merger or takeover situation is to make assessments and draw conclusions about the other culture. For the majority of employees, assessments made prior to any actual physical or socio-cultural integration are likely to be based on rumour, second-hand reporting, implicit theories and involve inference rather than first-hand knowledge or experience. When the partnering organization is also foreign, assessment of the other culture is likely to be conflated by perceived national stereotypes. For example, in the 12 months leading up to the legal announcement of a recent UK merger, many employees when questioned were unable to give consistent and accurate basic information as to the number of people employed by the partnering organization or their site locations. Furthermore, it was found that perceptions of what the other organization was like were largely based on impressions extrapolated from national brand advertising.

Gaining more factually based knowledge about the acquiring organization or other merger partner and its culture is one way of reducing the perceived threat and critical mass of the unknown. Such information is now always forthcoming from official sources within the organization at this time, however, this does not preclude the individual from finding out more for himself. Company reports, product literature, supplier/customer research directories, such as Kompass, are often more reliable sources of information than in-house rumours of local newspapers.

Research into the impact of culture change on the individual (Cartwright & Cooper, 1989; 1992) has shown that the experience is not always negative but depends on (i) the extent to which the individual values his own culture and (ii) his perception of the degree of attractiveness of the new or other culture. In other words, the experience is likely to lead to increased job satisfaction if valued aspects of the existing culture (i.e. rituals, practices, procedures, etc.) are accommodated and retained, and are supplemented by or integrated with the more desirable aspects of the culture of the combining organization.

Because, from the outset, mergers and acquisitions are invariably responded to as win/lose situations, there is a collective tendency for individuals to fight for and resist change in every area of organizational activity for fear of conceding ground to the other. In such situations, working alone or with your immediate work group, it can help to give some thought to the following questions:

What things about your current organization (i.e. values, systems, practices, managerial style, etc.) would you not like to see changed?

What things about your current organization would you like to see changed or may even in the past have tried to change but have been unsuccessful?

What are the main areas for improvement?

What do you *actually* know about the acquiring organization or other merger partner? What would you like to know?

What do you expect will change?

What do you *hope* will change?

In completing this exercise, you have now identified the potential areas of change which are likely to cause you anxiety and possibly stress, as well as the area where you would positively welcome change. Consequently, you are starting to move from a negative and resistant psychological state to a healthier more positive and rational negotiation mode which will be beneficial in responding to and discussing any proposed changes in the future. The maintenance of a flexible as opposed to a rigid mental attitude is important in reducing the stress response.

A number of more progressive organizations, with whom we have worked in such situations, have conducted large-scale acquisition/merger surveys to ascertain employee response to questions similar to those posed in this exercise. This information has proved extremely valuable in guiding integration decisions and creating an agenda for negotiation and discussion.

Maintaining life as normal. Robert Frost once wrote, 'The reason why worry kills more people than work is that more people worry than work.' Certainly, all of us at some time or another spend a considerable amount of unproductive time worrying and agonizing over events which never actually happen. As parents of teenage children, we worry about their possible drug involvement, yet the overwhelming majority of teenagers still reach adulthood without ever having experimented with drugs. Similarly, parental concern about juvenile crime has reached hysterical levels, yet reported crime statistics show that over the last few years there has actually been a reduction in juvenile crime.
Awareness as to the potential danger or threat of a situation is a more constructive alternative to turning a blind eye or naivety, but it is qualitatively different from worry. Worry is a consuming, often paralysing and dysfunctional emotion which serves no constructive purpose and results in stress.

As already discussed, to be able to deal with merger stress more effectively and so reduce its potentially negative impact, it is important to be able to switch off to rumours and maintain a balanced perspective. Rumours stem from collective insecurity. Often there are so many contradictory merger rumours circulating that rationally they could not possibly all be true. Deliberately avoiding or limiting the time spent engaging in or listening to rumour sessions at work and focusing on more immediate work or life goals is a desirable strategy. Avoidance behaviour, such as taking a walk at lunchtime or playing a game of squash rather than sitting around in the canteen discussing the merger with co-workers and risking becoming further depressed, not only provides a useful way of switching off to work but also has the advantage of improving physical health.

If you become aware of a persistent and concerning rumour which directly affects your work, take steps to confront it with your superior or union representative. Ask them for any specific information which they may have about the situation – what do they know? – rather than seeking their subjective opinion – what do they think? – or canvassing them for other rumours they might have heard. They may be able to allay your fears, though more often than not they will be as much in the dark as yourself. If so, it is important to accept that as the situation, rather than automatically assume that they know something but are not prepared to tell you and so increase your paranoia. Managers should recognize that they have a responsibility to regularly and consistently brief their subordinates on merger-related matters, even if the content of that briefing is only to re-affirm that, at the current time, there is little or no information to communicate.

Many employees in takeover and merger situations feel that they and their jobs are on trial and so become obsessed with their own survival. As a result, they will often act to promote a desirable image of themselves which they consider might impress those whom they perceive to be influential in the decision-making process. Typical behavioural manifestations are working longer hours, piling their desks with files, playing politics, belittling the contribution of others and generally getting themselves noticed. The effort, pretence and often social isolation of affecting or exaggerating behaviours which are uncharacteristic of the individual are likely to be stressful and have detrimental long-term psychological consequences. Furthermore, in the long term, they are likely to serve no useful purpose whatsoever, in that they may be misdirected towards the wrong decision-makers. Alternatively, the transparency of such behaviour will become recognized for what it is and will either be ignored or despised. It is far better to maintain a flexible and open mind, but at the same time remain true to yourself, than attempt to read (and possibly misread) the situation, and so be forever adjusting your behaviour in what is likely to be an unstable and changing environment.

Finally, whilst work routines may have been disrupted, it is important to maintain one's non-work and health routines.

Dealing With Sexual Harassment

Jane is a single parent with two teenage children. She is the sole breadwinner in her family. She works in the laboratory of a large chemical company. She is very ambitious and has been attending college in the evening to attain more qualifications. She has always got on well with her boss and is very pleased when he asks her if she would like to attend a European conference with him. Over dinner on the last evening of the conference, he hints that there is a promotion coming up in the department and that Jane may be a potential candidate. A male colleague, Eric, is also a possible candidate. Whilst less able and less committed to his job than Jane, he has been with the company six months longer than Jane. Jane's boss suggests that he could swing the decision her way if she would be prepared to sleep with him that night. Does she go along with him or say no and so risk losing her job and her only source of income?

Mary works as a motor mechanic. All her co-workers are male. The walls of the workplace are cluttered with sexually explicit posters and pictures. Frequently, the men make jokes and rude comments about Mary's physical attributes and appearance, comparing her with the women in the photographs. They clearly seem to think it's all a bit of harmless fun, but for Mary it's no joking matter. She comes to dread going to work. She wants to leave but wonders if she will find things much the same in any other garage.

The above scenarios are examples of sexual harassment and illustrate the two types of sexual harassment:

- Quid pro quo harassment or sexual blackmail – one thing in return for another (Jane's experience).
- Environmental harassment – where the effect of the conduct creates hostility and harms the victim's working environment, even though no tangible employment benefits have been lost (Mary's experience).

The term 'sexual harassment' was only devised in the 1970s. However, sexual harassment is essentially a new label for an old problem, in that many women of earlier generations have found themselves the recipients of *unwanted sexual attention* at work. Sexual harassment is not only demeaning, but as Jane's case clearly illustrates, it deprives women of opportunities that are available to men without sexual conditions. It is recognized that the potential victims of sexual harassment are not exclusively females. Men, particularly homosexual males, ethnic minorities and males working in predominately female work environments are also vulnerable to unwanted sexual attention. However, according to a recent UK survey (Phillips, Stockdale & Joeman, 1989), women are seven to eight times more likely to experience sexual harassment than men. Furthermore, whereas the sexual harassment of males is generally confined to verbal abuse and suggestive remarks, women are more likely to also experience some form of physical contact. Therefore, this section will focus primarily on the problem of sexual harassment and its associated stress as it affects women. However, much of the advice given will have equal application to men who may find themselves in this situation.

The evidence suggests that sexual harassment at work is a serious and growing problem. Rather than an unexpected work event, sexual harassment in the workplace would actually appear to be relatively commonplace. This may be a reflection of more enlightened social attitudes towards the discussion of such a topic. It may also reflect the growing number of women entering the workforce, particularly in non-traditional work roles and occupations, and the difficulties and problems that such changes in status present in the work environment.

Research trends
One of the earliest surveys was conducted in the USA by a popular women's magazine, *Redbook*, in 1976. The results were staggering in that 88% of 9,000 female respondents reported that they had experienced sexual harassment at work. A subsequent study undertaken by the United States Merit Systems Protection Board (1980) of 23,000 federal employees found that 42% of the women surveyed had experienced some form of sexual harassment within a two-year period (1978 -- 80). The USMSPB repeated the study in 1988 by sending a questionnaire to 13,000 federal employees. The results obtained were almost identical.

There have been a number of generally smaller-scale UK studies which have also produced some disturbing results. In 1981, the Liverpool branch of NALGO surveyed its members and found that 55% of women had experienced sexual harassment either in their current or previous jobs. Evidence from a study of women in West Yorkshire sponsored by the Equal Opportunities Commission found that 59% of women had been sexually harassed. In 1987, the Labour Research Department's survey reported a figure of 73%. A similar figure was reported by the National Association of School Teachers/Union of Women Teachers who conducted a survey in Birmingham secondary schools in the same year. More recently, a survey of 1,000 workers in Britain (Phillips, Stockdale & Joeman, 1989), which involved 800 women and 200 men, found that 16% of women and 2% of men reported sexual harassment in their current job. In 1991, in a survey undertaken for the Alfred Marks Bureau of the employment agency's clients, 47% of women and 14% of men stated that they had been sexually harassed.

Similar studies conducted in various European countries suggest that the problem of sexual harassment is widespread and not culturally specific. For example, a survey of 4,200 secretaries in West Germany conducted by *Brigette* magazine reported that 54% had been sexually harassed. Another study, commissioned by the Netherlands government and conducted by the University of Groningen (1986) found that 58% of women questioned had experienced sexual harassment at work.

Whilst these surveys appear to differ considerably in terms of their estimates of the magnitude of the problem from 16% to 88%, the differences can be accounted for by a number of factors. These factors include differences in sample sizes, sampling techniques, differences in the questions asked (e.g. some surveys have asked about experiences in current jobs, others have asked about previous as well as current jobs) and the degree of consciousness of sexual harassment as a concept and awareness as to its constituent behaviours. For example, the USA was the first country to introduce administrative regulations and judicial recognition that sexual harassment is unlawful sex discrimination. Therefore, one would expect that individuals within that country would have a more heightened awareness of the concept than some European countries, where sexual harassment has not been thought of as falling within the intended scope of discrimination law. Nevertheless, despite the varying estimates, the evidence is sufficiently consistent to confirm that sexual harassment is a real and pervasive problem in the workplace.

The impact of sexual harassment

Sexual attraction between men and women often occurs in the workplace. Provided this attraction is mutual and there is no abuse of power, the relationship may be distracting, but it is not necessarily a problem. The behaviours associated with sexual attraction, what have been termed the 'courting cues' (Cohen, 1983), may take the form of sexual innuendo, staring, unnecessary touching, patting, etc. and may be similar to those behaviours which constitute sexual harassment. However, sexual harassment differs from

sexual attraction in that these behaviours are unwelcome
and unacceptable to the recipient. According to a report
issued by the Commission of the European Communities in
1988: 'The essential feature of sexual harassment is that it is
one-sided, uninvited or imposed.'

There are many definitions of the kinds of behaviour
which may be described as sexual harassment. These fall
into three broad categories – verbal, physical and visual –
and include the following conduct:

Verbal conduct	Physical conduct	Visual conduct
– propositions, requests or demands for sexual favours – pressure for sexual activity – offensive flirtations – suggestive remarks – innuendoes or lewd comments – tricks or jokes of a sexual nature – offensive comments about appearance or dress – derogatory or degrading abuse	– staring or leering – gestures – unnecessary touching, patting or pinching or brushing against another employee's body – wolf whistles	– displays of pornographic pictures or other sexually suggestive or derogatory objects, pictures or written materials

Source: Commission of the European Communities

However, it is obvious that merely producing a litany of
behaviours which may be regarded as sexual harassment
does not provide any clear definition of the term. Different
women may regard the same conduct as tolerable or offensive. Individual women may regard the same conduct by different men differently. A woman may find it acceptable for a
close male colleague to occasionally put his arm around her,
but that does not give *all* the males she works with licence to
do the same. Therefore, whether or not a behaviour constitutes sexual harassment is defined by the *response* of the
recipient rather than the *intention* of the perpetrator.

Despite the prevalence of sexual harassment in the workplace, few women make any formal complaint. Indeed, many organizations still perceive sexual harassment to be an individual's rather than an organizational problem. It has been estimated that as few as one in a thousand harassed women are likely to file any formal complaint (Colatosi & Karg, 1992). Typically, reluctance to report the incident stems from fear of retaliation and/or fear of loss of privacy. Many victims also consider that if they were to make any formal complaint, it would be criticized and not taken seriously.

However, the outcomes of sexual harassment are far from trivial. As Renee Goldsmith Kasinky (1972), Associate Professor of Criminal Justice at the University of Massachusetts, puts it: 'Sexual harassment may be one of the most widespread occupational health hazards women face, as well as the best-guarded secret.'

Response to sexual harassment is not dissimilar from response to rape. According to J.W. Jensen and Barbara Gutek (1982), surveyed victims of sexual harassment report having experienced disgust (80%), anger (68%) and depression (20%). Sexual harassment is associated with a range of negative outcomes involving deterioration in work performance, psychological and physical health, affective feelings towards job and relationships with others at work (Crull, 1982; Gutek, 1985). For example, the USMSPB study (1980) found that one-third of women who had been sexually harassed felt that their emotional or physical condition had been adversely affected by the experience. Crull (1982) found that 75% of victims reported a decrease in work performance, 90% reported a deterioration in psychological health and 63% a deterioration in physical health.

Studies have shown that the majority of women initially respond to sexual harassment by either ignoring the incident and doing nothing about it, or attempting to avoid the harasser. If the behaviour persists and/or the working environment becomes intolerable and stressful, many women feel forced to leave the organization or ask for a transfer to another department. Crull (1982) reports that as many as

42% of the victims in her survey had resigned from jobs because of sexual harassment. A further 25% of those sampled had been fired or laid off as a result of sexual harassment.

Aside from the adverse impact this may have on the victim's career and self-image, such actions are costly to organizations. The US Merit Systems Protection Board found that sexual harassment at work, in terms of recruitment and retraining costs alone, cost the US Federal Government $189 million over a two-year period from May 1978 to 1980. In a wider context, the sudden and often ill-explained decision to quit reinforces the stereotype of women as unreliable workers and negatively affects future career prospects.

Stopping sexual harassment

There are a range of possible responses to sexual harassment. Typically, these fall into two categories; actions which lead to a change in behaviour in the harassed individual, and actions which confront or attempt to change the behaviour of the harasser.

Avoidance or action to reduce exposure to risk. As discussed, the majority of victims of sexual harassment decide to remove themselves from the situation by leaving the organization or transferring to another department. Such behaviour is usually preceded by attempts to avoid or ignore the harasser and staying cool, in the hope that the harasser will get the message that the victim is not interested. Such tactics are invariably unsuccessful, as evidenced by the number of women who ultimately feel forced to resign.

Sexual harassment requires quick action on the part of the victim. Otherwise, it does not go away but usually gets worse. Attempting to ignore rather than confront the offensive behaviour can lead to misunderstanding and confusing messages. Passivity may be interpreted as acquiescence and encouragement rather than rejection. It may also even work against the women should she decide to file a formal complaint at some later date.

Alternatively, some individuals may respond by changing or altering aspects of themselves – their behaviour, their appearance or their clothes – because they feel that they may have inadvertently encouraged the harasser in some way, by being overly friendly or too overtly attractive. Again, this strategy is likely to prove unsuccessful in deterring the harasser and may only serve to fuel negative self-feelings within the victim. According to Phillips, Stockdale & Joeman (1989), 11% of victims consider themselves to be partly at fault by failing to be assertive or inadvertently encouraging comments or advances.

It has to be recognized that sexual harassment is not motivated by physical attraction or sexual desire, but by power and/or male confusion between a woman's sex and work role and expected behaviour.

The dominant theories attribute sexual harassement as being:

1. the result of unequal distribution of power between the sexes and therefore part of the 'continuum of male-aggressive, female-passive patterns' (Medea & Thompson, 1974), or
2. the carry-over into the workplace of gender-based expectations for behaviour that are irrelevant or inappropriate to work, whereby a woman's work role is confused with her sex role. For example, a male boss may expect female subordinates to be pleased by his flirtatious comments and behaviours in the same way as a wife or girlfriend.

Consequently, the likelihood of being sexually harassed is more the outcome of the woman's status or role, rather than the way she looks or behaves, and is unlikely to be deterred by any overt or deliberate suppression of sexuality. Hence women in non-traditional occupations, of low status in the organization (i.e. part-time workers), highly educated women, or women who are perceived to be more vulnerable because of their status in society (i.e. single parents, divorcees, widows and ethnic minorities) face an increased risk of sexual harassment (US Merit Systems Protection Board, 1980).

Therefore, strategies which aim to avoid or reduce exposure to risk by changing the behaviour of the harassed individual are characteristically ineffective and often costly in both financial and humanistic terms. They not only fail to present a satisfactory solution to the harassed individual but allow the perpetrator the opportunity to continue the offensive behaviour.

Physical reaction. P.B. Bart (1981) interviewed women who had been raped and those to had avoided rape, and concluded that those who avoided rape were more likely to have screamed and physically struggled as opposed to talking or pleading. This would seem to suggest that some form of physical reaction (i.e. a sharp slap, a shove away or the removal of an offending hand) may stop any further advances. However, such actions are not without their dangers, particularly if the individual is alone with the harasser. Also, as was found in the above study, physical responses often need to be supplemented by other strategies.

Confrontation. Ignoring, giggling, smiling, disapproving frowns or embarrassed looks, because they send mixed signals, are open to misinterpretation, and so often are ineffective in stopping unwanted sexual advances. Ridiculing the harasser or making a joke of the incident may work sometimes, but making light of or appearing to trivialize the matter and so deny its seriousness may also escalate the situation or lead to retaliation. The more effective strategy requires a clear, consistent and assertive response which leaves the harasser in no doubt that their behaviour is unacceptable. Responding assertively involves:

1. Looking the harasser straight in the eyes.
2. A firm and calm tone of voice.
3. A clear statement as to why and what it is about the

behaviour that is unacceptable and what you want the harasser to do or not to do. Colatosi and Karg (1992) suggest that positive commands ('I want you to keep your hands to yourself') work better than negative commands ('I don't want you to touch me'). They also suggest that it is useful to describe in words what is happening while it is happening ('You have your hand on my left breast; I want you to remove it *now*) or to repeat aloud any sexual requests made.

4. Finally, telling the individual what you propose to do if the behaviour continues, e.g. file a formal complaint.

Internal report. Externalizing and telling others about the incident is preferable to trying to ignore it or to pretend it never happened. Often, the victim is not the man's only target, and sharing information is an effective way in which to build up a case against the perpetrator. A group complaint is more powerful than one from a single individual. Telling or enlisting help from friends, co-workers or spouse is a means of gaining support and advice which may make the victim feel better. But direct action to address and arrest the problem requires a formal report to a supervisor, manager, trade union representative or other company official. If the harasser is one's boss, such reports should be made to his immediate superior. The decision to report should be made as soon as possible after the incident has occurred. The victim should formally record the time, the place and the specific details of the offensive behaviour and whether there were any witnesses. When the harasser is confronted his first reaction is likely to be to deny it; it is therefore helpful for those investigating the incident to be able to direct the discussion towards specific allegations. The victim should avoid procrastination. The evidence presented by Professor Anita Hill in her recent case against US Supreme Court nominee Clarence Thomas was very much weakened by the fact that 10 years had elapsed before she made the information public.

Many large organizations have incorporated policies and

procedures relating to sexual harassment; however, the absence of any formal policy should not deter a report. The climate towards sexual harassment is considerably more sympathetic than it was in the past. Many trade unions, for example the Council of Civil Service Unions, the National Union of Public Employees and the Amalgamated Engineering Union, provide awareness education, training and guidelines to local union representatives as to how to deal sensitively and effectively with reports of sexual harassment.

External report. In a recent survey conducted in Spain (UGT, 1987) of over 7,000 working women, it was found that 33% thought that there was no legal remedy for sexual harassment and 43% were unaware of what legal remedy there was or how to have recourse to it.

If the harassment takes the form of sexual assault, the victim has remedies under criminal law and can report the matter to the police. In the UK, as yet, there is no specific law relating to sexual harassment. However, cases of sexual harassment have been successfully brought to court under the provisions of the Sex Discrimination Act 1975. The first sexual harassment case, Strathclyde Regional Council v. Porcelli, came before the Scottish courts in 1986 and involved sexual harassment by the woman's male colleagues. Such behaviour included suggestive remarks and brushing up against the complainant. The claim that such behaviour constituted unlawful discrimination, on the grounds that because of her gender, Mrs Porcelli had been treated unfavourably, was upheld and an award of £3,000 was made in favour of Mrs Porcelli and against her employer. As well as cases brought directly under the Sex Discrimination Act, sexual harassment, if it results in resignation or dismissal, has been recognized as valid grounds for claiming unfair or constructive dismissal under Section 52(2)(c) of the Employment Protection (Consolidation) Act. Such actions, if successful, result in an award for damages against the organization, not against the perpetrator. Advice concerning legal action is available from the Equal Opportunites Commission.

There are other external agencies which offer help to victims of sexual harassment. Women Against Sexual Harassment (WASH) provides free and confidential advice to anyone who has been sexually harassed at work. In addition to general legal and employment advice, it will also provide support and counselling (the address is given in the references to this chapter). Support and counselling is also available from local rape crisis centres. As mentioned earlier, the emotional response to sexual harassment is often similar to that following rape, and trained rape counsellors can be extremely helpful in assisting women work through these negative emotions.

Choosing the right option
Any decision to take legal action should probably be regarded as a last resort. Any legal proceedings are likely to be lengthy, contested and if successful will result in eventual reinstatement and/or a financial award for damages. The major disadvantage is that, at present, such hearings are public and the anticipation of a court appearance is itself likely to be stressful. Whilst the existence of legal sanctions is of paramount importance in emphasizing to organizations the serious nature of sexual harassment, in terms of personal solutions to the problem, other options are better pursued at the outset.

Confrontation is the most effective initial option for a variety of reasons:

1. it communicates a clear message that the behaviour is unacceptable and not to be repeated
2. if the act was motivated by power, confronting and challenging the behaviour upsets the traditional continuum of aggressive-male, passive-female patterns of behaviour. The disequilibrium this creates is unlikely to be shocking. In behaving assertively, the individual is likely to feel more confident and in control of the situation and to be perceived by the harasser as less vulnerable and powerless; particularly if the woman

147

makes it clear that she will not hesitate to take official action if the behaviour continues.

3. alternatively, if the behaviour was the outcome of inappropriate male expectations of the female role in the workplace, or role confusion, then it directly confronts this issue and creates an opportunity for role clarification and negotiation. Often only by confrontation can a woman create an atmosphere in which she can feel comfortable stating exactly what she does or does not find to be acceptable work-related behaviour. For example, a female engineer who finds herself at the receiving end of suggestive comments might wish to restate and remind her male colleagues that she is employed as an engineer and not as a woman, and therefore she would like her colleagues to limit their comments to business-related issues.

Paula Popovich and Betty Licata (1987) suggest that role negotiation techniques (RNT) can play a useful part in decreasing the opportunity for a person's sex role and work role to become confused, and so prevent sexual harassment. They suggest that such techniques should be periodically employed in organizations, before any incident has taken place. The technique involves each member of the work group listing on paper (often anonymously) what he or she feels the other members should do more of or better, what they should do less of, and what needs to change. These comments then form the basis for group negotiation, and a final written contract is drawn up which details the work roles and expectations of group members. Periodic checks can then be made on the members via appraisals.

Whether an individual decides to take further action and make a formal report of the incident will depend on the particular circumstances. However, it is the individual's interest to keep her own record of the incident and perhaps, informally, report the matter to a colleague. Any recurrence should then automatically be both confronted and formally reported through internal channels.

In more general terms, action can be taken by individuals within organizations to address the potential problem of sexual harassment in the workplace by lobbying for the introduction of formal policies and procedures and the provision of awareness/education training programmes. Assertiveness training can also be extremely helpful in developing the skills of the individual in coping with such situations and handling the power dynamics of the workplace more generally.

Coping With Redundancy

> Peter Hardy, a bank manager, threw himself off cliffs at Beachy Head, in East Sussex, after being made redundant from Barclays. Mr Hardy 45, of Speen, Buckinghamshire, who joined Barclays when he was 18, drove to the cliffs two days after being offered early retirement, an inquest in Eastbourne was told. Coroner's verdict: suicide.

This poignant extract, from *The Times*, 12 March 1993, illustrates a desperate response to a situation which has become increasingly more commonplace in recent years. That Peter Hardy, a relatively young man with possibly 20 or 30 years of active life still ahead of him, should chose to end his life so prematurely encapsulates the extreme misery and sense of rejection that many people experience following job loss, and the importance and meaning which work gives to an individual's life.

Whilst the primary motive to work is invariably monetary, for the vast majority of the population having job is more than just having a source of income. Studies which have examined the reasons why people go to work (Warr, 1982) have found that 69% of men and 65% of women in the UK workforce would continue to work even if they found themselves in a situation in which there was no financial necessity to do so. Work serves a variety of functions for the individuals:

- it imposes a time structure on the day
- it provides an opportunity to use existing skills and acquire new ones
- it provides the opportunity for interpersonal contact with people outside the family
- it provides activity and variety
- it gives the individual goals and purposes
- it defines aspects of personal status and identity.

Consequently, when an individual loses a job, the sense of loss experienced extends beyond the forfeiture of a regular pay cheque.

Unemployment increases the individual's dependency on others, both physically and psychologically. Not only does the individual have to come to terms with living on a reduced income – estimated to be typically between 45% and 60% of employed salary – but he also has to accept that he is no longer responsible for the provision of that income but is dependent on others (i.e. the state, family members, financial institutions, money lenders, etc.).

Characteristically, unemployment presents a range of common problems which are a potential source of distress to the individual. Firstly, there are problems of *loss of identity*. In personal and societal terms, a job defines who you are, where you live, the people you mix with and your status in society generally. Women who voluntarily leave their jobs to become full-time mothers frequently report experiencing not dissimilar problems concerning loss of job-derived identity. From the outset, giving birth is a significant social leveller. To midwives, health visitors and concomitant hospital staff, all women who have babies are undifferentiated and responded to as mothers; previous career and occupational status is of little or no importance. For the career woman who decides to stay at home with her young family, this newly defined identity of 'mother' in some way displaces and erases whatever went before. For many women, the reclassification of being '*just* a housewife', to talking about what she was in terms of what work she used to do, as if it were a previous incarnation, requires considerable adjustment. However, the birth of a baby does automatically confer a new role and job of work, which although it may have less status and be less socially valued provides activity and purpose. Unfortunately, the same cannot be said for redundancy.

Because of the loss of temporal structure, activity and purpose provided by work, unemployed people often become demotivated and have great difficulty in filling their day. Consequently, as research has shown, they spend a great deal of time watching TV, sleeping and sitting around. The limited availability of money restricts the opportunity for activity and special contact outside the home, and as a result frequently places a considerable strain on family relationships.

One of the most difficult problems faced by the unemployed is coping with the *uncertainty* of the situation. When an individual is made redundant, there is no way of knowing how long it will be before he finds another job. This presents major dilemmas, especially concerning decisions to cut back on expenses, such as trading down to a smaller house or moving to a less desirable suburb. The maintenance of an existing lifestyle by borrowing or using redundancy payments may prove ultimately disastrous if unemployment becomes long-term. Similarly, the panic selling of assets in a falling or depressed market may be costly and result in unnecessary distress if the individual is able to gain re-employment in a relatively short period of time.

Uncertain job future can have a serious impact on *self-esteem*. Any initial optimism is likely to be soon eroded in the face of a rising pile of rejected job applications, particularly in a recessionary job market. Fears develop that existing skills will deteriorate over time if not used, and self-esteem and confidence decline. As high unemployment rates have increasingly become a feature of the UK economy in recent years, the social stigma attached to unemployment has become less marked than it was. However, particularly amongst older workers and those made redundant for the first time, there still remain the cultural remnants of a strong work ethic, which cause people to feel guilty or apologetic about not having a job.

Therefore, whilst for some, redundancy may present a blessed relief from the tedium of a boring, dissatisfying or physically debilitating job, it is for many a major life event with unprecedented negative financial, physical and psychological consequences. As research has consistently demonstrated, whilst work may be stressful, having no work is even more stressful. Evidence from studies conducted by Professor Peter Warr and his colleagues at Sheffield University (Warr, 1987) has found that employed people are on average psychologically and physically more healthy than those who are unemployed. The impact of job loss on mental health is typically rapid. Within three months, mental well-being is significantly impaired and subsequently stabilizes rather than continuing to decline after a six-month period of unemployment. Furthermore, compared with employed men, the evidence suggests that unemployed men are significantly more likely to die in the course of the following decade; the differential probability being particularly marked for suicide and death from lung cancer.

Recent unemployment trends indicate that job losses tend to be heaviest amongst older workers, who also find it most difficult to find new employment (Social Trends, 1990). Approximately 60% of males in the age range 50 – 59 and 35% of males aged 35 – 49 remain unemployed for two years or more, compared with 23% of males aged 25 – 34 (Holmes & Cartwright, 1993). The chances of gaining employment are greater for female workers. At least 50% of all women under 50 remain unemployed for less than 26 weeks. Compared with men, women are more likely to take up part-time or lower-paid jobs.

The disproportionate burden of job losses borne by older workers may be explained by their over-representation in long-established declining industries (such as primary and

manufacturing), their under-representation in new and ex-
panding industries, and the tendency of employers to dis-
miss older workers in all industries. The impact of
redundancy tends to be hardest felt by single persons, single-
income families and especially the middle-aged. For those in
mid-life, the event often corresponds with other lifestage
crises. The redundant middle manager in his early forties
probably still has dependent children to support, yet his
chances of gaining re-employment, compared to a younger
man, are perceived to be less, as he is more likely to encounter the problem of ageism and is frequently less geographically mobile. Similarly, compared with those over
fifty, he is likely to be less well cushioned financially, and
too young to take early retirement.

Earlier in this chapter, we discussed the individual's response to merger and acquisition in the context of the four-
stage bereavement model. This model is equally appropriate
in understanding how individuals respond to job loss, even
when they are made redundant from jobs which they did not
find particularly enjoyable. Because the time spent at work
consumes so much of our daily lives, for most people its loss
creates as great a void as the loss of a close family member
or friend. Max Eggert, an outplacement consultant, in his recent book, *Outplacement: A Guide to Management and Delivery*, relates the story of how Margaret Thatcher, on losing
the premiership, felt so lost without her usual tightly packed
timetable that she even became confused about what day it
was.

Coping with the shock – the early days

Whilst we will focus on the more practical aspects of redundancy and job search, it is important to be aware of the
emotional cycle associated with the event. The initial sur-
prise or *shock* of redundancy invariably causes the individual to freeze up and be unable to make any plans. Often
the response is to minimalize or trivialize the event. Many
people on being made redundant respond by taking a holiday or going on a spending spree, as if to convince themselves or those around them of the insignificance of the

event. They may even procrastinate about seeking advice or signing on for benefits. From initial shock will come *anger and bitterness*. Much of this anger will be outwardly directed; resentment towards one's former employer, family and friends, particularly if they have well paid or satisfying jobs. This stage often represents a high-energy period, when the individual will be prone to sudden and frequent outbursts of temper or will frantically apply for any kind of job which might be going, irrespective of whether he meets the criteria or not. Irrationally, the individual may expect a call from his former employer contritely offering him his old job back, having realized that it was a mistake to let him go.

In order to cope better with this difficult period, it is important for the individual to recognize that the feelings he is experiencing are normal and in time can be worked through. During the early days, the individual should accept that intuitively he is likely to behave irrationally. Therefore, the following tips are useful:

- It is most important to keep reminding one's self that it is *jobs* not *people* that are made redundant. Jobs may become valueless and obsolete but people don't. Rather than a crisis, redundancy can turn out to be an opportunity. Even the Prime Minister, John Major, had a period of unemployment in his career.
- Don't panic and risk acting with unnecessary haste. Allow some time to calm down and get over the initial shock. A few days away and a change of scene may help, however, it is a far better idea to plan to take a holiday *after* you have found a new job or at least have a clearer idea of your future plans.
- Inform your building society or bank that you have been made redundant. As unemployment has escalated, financial institutions have developed a more sympathetic attitude towards borrowers who find themselves in this situation and are prepared to negotiate financial arrangements. Foreclosure is not an imminent problem in the early days following redundancy, so don't make yourself ill worrying about it!

■ Do not procrastinate about signing on or making enquiries about available state benefits. They system was
intended as a safeguard to help people in this situation.
You have paid hard-earned contributions whilst in work
so there is no need to feel ashamed about using a service you have helped to fund. Most people do not expect their home to burn down and be made homeless,
yet if such a situation should happen, they do not feel
embarrassed about making an insurance claim. In principle, the social security system operates in a similar
way as an insurance policy to protect the individual
from unfortunate and unintended life accidents and
hazards.

■ Be open to others about your situation; they may prove
helpful in providing you with contacts that may lead to
a job. Contact with others in the same predicament,
through a job club or similar self-help group, can also be
a valuable means of social support. However, joining
such a group in the very early days, when one is still extremely angry and bitter, may be counterproductive in
further fuelling or prolonging that anger or leading to
depression.

■ In order to commence your job search, you will need to
prepare a curriculum vitae (c.v.). Many individuals find
this difficult to do in the early days following redundancy, or make a poor attempt. There are a number of
possible reasons for this:

(i) having received a major blow to their self-confidence
and self-esteem, they do not feel sufficiently positive
about themselves to present themselves in a way which
will impress potential employees

(ii) it may be such a long time since they last had to prepare a c.v., they lack the necessary skills

(iii) in preparing a c.v., the individual is forced to make
a public admission that he is without a job.

Therefore, rather than immediately rushing to the
typewriter to document your work history, it is important firstly to conduct the kind of personal stock-take

outlined in the earlier section of this chapter (refer to Coping With Mergers and Acquisitions) to assess one's strength and weaknesses. Asking people around you who know you well for their opinions can be helpful in this regard. Documenting previous achievements can be beneficial in that it helps the individual to recall times when they felt good about themselves. Reliving past successes or giving oneself what are good 'positive strokes' has enormous psychological value. It is often also useful to ask others about the kind of jobs they think you might be good at.

- Finally, resist the temptation to apply for each and every job advertised regardless of its suitability. When it comes to finding a job, the number of interviews/ offers you are likely to receive does not increase proportionately to the number of applications made, particularly if you disregard or fail to meet the criteria specified. Rather, it will result in a disproportionate number of depressing rejections, particularly if the c.v. is rushed and ill-prepared, which will only serve to further and unnecessarily erode self-confidence.

Coping in the longer term

As we have already discussed in earlier sections, anger is a counterproductive emotion, and the sooner this is recognized, vented and exhausted the better. Whilst the individual remains fixated at this stage, he is most unlikely to make any positive and realistic career plans. Even if he is fortunate enough to obtain a job interview, he is liable to communicate this anger to the interviewer to negative effect. Anger is followed by depression. Sometimes depression is preceded by what is termed the 'fantasy effect' or avoidance behaviour, whereby the individual mentally focuses on 'rescue scenarios'. Such scenarios are either unlikely to happen (i.e. getting one's old job back, winning the pools) or represent situations which the individual is not prepared to act upon (i.e. alternative career ideas, such as setting up one's own business). Temporarily, such fantasies can be comforting to the individual and are a way of avoiding the reality of seeking work and so risking rejection. Anger, fantasy and depression are also normal responses in the emotional cycle. However, if the individual remains in any of these states for a long period of time, he should not hesitate to seek professional counselling.

As the number of pre-retirement courses now available indicates, it has become increasingly recognized that even giving up a job voluntarily requires systematic preparation and professional counselling if the individual is to cope effectively and adjust to the change in lifestyle. Redundancy requires a similar approach which extends beyond a sympathetic attitude and a copy of the Situations Vacant section of the daily newspaper. In recognition, many more progressive large organizations now provide what are termed 'outplacement' facilities to support and counsel individuals who are compelled to leave their employer to achieve the next stage of their career. Such facilities vary in terms of the standard, type of service and assistance they provide. They may be run in-house or be provided by external outplacement consultants, of which there are currently over 120 in the UK. Such services are often quite expensive and are frequently restricted to fairly senior personnel. However, on being made redundant it is worthwhile asking the organization what assistance they can provide. It may only be to agree to allow you to continue to use your company car for the next month, whilst you sort yourself out.

In this section, we suggest a variety of positive steps which will help the individual to move through the job-less cycle.

Preparing a systematic job search campaign

Consider all possibilities. If an individual has been made redundant from a declining industry it stands to reason that:

1. he is likely to find that alternative jobs will be difficult to find in that industry
2. any job opportunities which do arise will attract a large field of similarly placed candidates

3. if he is successfully re-employed in that industry and it continues to decline, he faces the likelihood of being made redundant yet again in the future.

It is therefore important to consider your job search, not just in the light of what work you have been doing, but also what you could or would like to be doing. Initial career decisions are typically based on incomplete information and often little real knowledge of what the day-to-day work involves. Early career choices are often influenced by factors such as parental or peer pressure, images portrayed by the media, high-starting salaries and attractive perks or glossy recruitment literature, rather than aptitude and personality. Career satisfaction is therefore more a matter of chance than choice. However, even if a good choice is made initially, over time a career can often become inappropriate or dissatisfying as different stages in the life cycle are reached and attitudes and values change. Redundancy can therefore present an opportunity for reappraisal, and a chance to make a fresh and invigorating new start.

Research (Holmes & Cartwright, 1993) indicates, particularly for those over 35, that the most popular career change is towards the autonomy of careers and jobs such as self-employment, lecturing, teaching or consultancy. Between 1979 and 1989, the number of self-employed people in the UK rose by over 70%, from just under 2 million to around 3.25 million. Many individuals who move to self-employment report substantially increased job satisfaction, especially if they are to turn a hobby into a job. Changing career may seem like an interesting but daunting prospect, yet tens of thousands of those who leave HM Forces each year have been successfully making that transition for years.

There are a variety of sources of information and career advice available other than job centres and job clubs:

(i) Career consultants
There are a number of private consultancy practices which offer careers guidance, usually run by or employing the services of an occupational psychologist. Typically, the

assessment and consultation process involves in-depth interviews and the completion of a series of psychometric tests and questionnaires to ascertain individual aptitudes and suitability for certain kinds of work or training. As well as advising on potential career paths, many outplacement organizations also provide advice and skill training on c.v. preparation, interview techniques, etc.

(ii) Local authority careers services

All large towns and cities have a careers service office which can be a useful source of information on jobs, training, university courses, etc. Many also provide specific adult guidance services. Local libraries are also potential sources of career information; many institutions of higher and further education run short courses which may be useful to the unemployed in areas of skills training, starting up a new business, etc. Help in this area is also available from local enterprise agencies or the Training and Enterprise Council (TEC).

(iii) Self-help manuals/courses

There are a number of helpful publications such as *Build your own Rainbow* (Hopson & Scally, 1984) and *What Color is your Parachute?* (Nelson-Bolles, 1989). The Open University also produces a relatively inexpensive self-development pack comprising workbooks, self-assessment questionnaires, etc. designed to help the individual to realize his potential.

Construct a c.v. Curricula vitae are vitally important as marketing tools in securing job interviews. In themselves they do not get jobs – people get jobs, not c.v.'s. As well as standard personal biographical information, the c.v. should include your work experience, beginning with your most recent employment; provide a summary of your educational qualifications, aptitudes, professional or trade associations and your interests; and give a statement of your achievements, both work- and non-work-related. In the USA, it is illegal for employers to ask age-related questions on application forms or at interviews. If you consider that disclosing your age may result in unfair discrimination, do not include it unless specifically directed to do so.

In the past, it was the convention to prepare a c.v. in a strictly chronological format. In recognition that the prime objective of the c.v. is to capture the interest of its recipient, more distinctive and dynamic alternative forms of c.v. have become recognized as being more effective. Those which provide a powerful up-front section which briefly summarizes experiences and achievements, and gives a kind of 20- to 30-second commercial or postcard-size advertisement of yourself can be particularly effective. Rather than ploughing through pages of historical information, they immediately provide the reader with pertinent information which captures his attention and alerts him to read on.

Again, there are a number of publications which provide useful guidance on preparing a c.v. For example, *Super Job Search* by Peter Studner (1989) is an excellent source for professionals and managers. However, a few basic tips are:

- A c.v. should not be too long – no more than three pages.
- It should be typewritten or handwritten in black pen, so that it can be easily photocopied by potential employers.
- Use short and punchy sentences; avoid jargon.
- Experiment with layout, headings, margins, etc. (software packages can be most useful in this regard).
- Say more about your recent work experiences and less the further back in the past you go.
- Always enclose with a covering letter. Putting your c.v. into a folder or clear perspex sleeve is also a good idea. It will ensure that it remains in the pristine condition it was in when it left your possession, and will prevent it from incurring accidental damage, coffee spills, etc. which may unfairly detract from its appearance.

Use alternative methods of job search. Apart from responding to advertised vacancies, it is important to be aware that nearly 70% of managerial jobs are never advertised. Networking (i.e. using informal contacts) or sending out speculative c.v.s directly to potential employers or recruitment agencies can extend possibilities.

Polish up interview techniques. The art of successful interviewing or being interviewed is an extensive enough topic in itself to be the subject of an entire book. Indeed, you will find many such books in your local bookshop, library or careers office. However, advance preparation is of fundamental importance. This means:

- Doing some prior research about the company – size, product range, locations, etc.
- Drawing up a list of questions you are expecting to be asked, including those questions that you would most not like to be asked (you can be fairly certain that a skilled interviewer will ask them!). Plan and then practice your answers with others in a role-play situation. Other people can provide useful feedback on how clear, convincing or enthusiastic your answers sound.
- Drawing up a list of questions you would like to ask.
- Always allowing plenty of contingency time so that you do not risk the possibility of arriving late for an interview. Take with you a spare copy of your c.v. in case it has been misplaced, and also so you can refer to it during the interview.

Coping emotionally

Many individuals on being made redundant would probably consider a systematic job search in itself a full-time job. However, almost everyone is likely to encounter periods when time hangs heavy. It is important to maintain the discipline of getting up reasonably early in the morning, getting dressed and planning the day's activities. Physical appearance can often become neglected when one spends most of the time at home and has little contact with people other than immediate family or friends. By investing in an answering machine, important job-related message will not be missed and yet the individual no longer feels so housebound that he cannot take himself out of the house. As research has shown, physical health often deterioriates following redundancy, and it is therefore important that the individual continues to eat sensibly and regularly and undertakes some form of physical exercise. Exercise is beneficial not only in improving physical fitness and providing an outlet for anger and aggressive feelings, but also in that the resultant improvement in body shape enhances self-image. Fears concerning the deterioration of existing skills, loss of purpose and social contact outside the house can often be overcome if the individual continues to work in a temporary, part-time or voluntary capacity. It is not that unusual for such activities to develop into full-time paid employment. Gaps in employment on c.v.s raise eyebrows; however, evidence that the individual has continued to work in a part-time or voluntary capacity or undertaken further training demonstrates motivation and commitment to maintain and develop skills. Working in a voluntary capacity with people less fortunate than oneself can also be extremely intrinsically rewarding and help the individual put his own situation into perspective.

One redundant executive tells the story of how he was successful in gaining an interview, but when the interviewer realized his age, he stated that he was really looking for a much younger man. The executive suggested that he would be willing to work on a stopgap basis until the organization found someone they considered more suitable. The organization agreed and ten months later, the executive was still working there and found himself being offered a permanent job. There has been an increasing trend towards temporary and stopgap managerial positions; a publication entitled *The Directory of Interim Management*, compiled by Robert Baird, 75 Manor Way, Blackheath, London, SE3, gives information on organizations who provide this service.

Coping With Unethical Behaviour in the Workplace

'This world only goes forward because of those who oppose it' (Goethe)

In a recent survey (Burke, Maddock & Rose, 1993), 43% of senior managers and professionals considered that being unfaithful to one's domestic partner was morally worse than tax fraud. Only 20% thought that tax faud was morally worse than partner infidelity. It is not the debate as to the relative moral superiority of these acts which is interesting, but the way in which these findings illustrate that individuals are willing to engage in that debate, thus confirming that people do discriminate between codes of behaviour and ethics appropriate to their personal life and those appropriate to business matters.

The issue of business ethics has fuelled considerable recent debate. Events such as the tragedy at Bhopal, the Exxon oil spill in Alaska, the Guinness affair, the BCCI fraud and the Maxwell pension fund scandal have raised the question, once again, of whether 'business ethics' and 'profit maximization' are two incompatible concepts. Certainly, the language of business equates the activity with game-playing; there are major players, winners and losers, mavericks, and those with a reputation for bending the rules, or bluffing and getting away with it, often seem to acquire the respect of other players. Consistent with the sporting analogy, those who draw attention to unethical practices or shout 'foul play' are described as *whistle-blowers*, implying that they stop the action and spoil the fun. Frequently, whistle-blowers in business games emerge, like their sporting equivalents on the playing fields, as the least popular characters in an organization. Underlying this analogy is the conscience-comforter, that if business is merely a game and the most important goal is to win, then any means by which this end is achieved are justified.

It has been argued that unethical behaviour is often a result of organizational culture, in terms of the pressure that

163

managers sometimes feel for performance measured solely in economics and competitive terms. However, not all immoral behaviour in the workplace is directed towards improving organizational performance, but is more concerned with lining the individual's pockets or with self-protection.

Thomas McCann tells the story of how, in the early 1950s, the management of an American company, the United Fruit Company, helped to overthrow the Guatemalan government in order to improve local business conditions. McCann, an employee at the time, was aware of this decision and yet did nothing about it because he was so closely involved with the company that he did not consider it to be a moral or ethical issue. Because he did not recognize the event as presenting a moral dilemma, the situation did not cause him stress at the time, but the fact that he has since openly talked about the issue presumably suggests that his behaviour retrospectively caused him some discomfort.

Relatively few individuals are likely to find themselves in situations where the questionable behaviour of members of their organization has such potentially dramatic consequences. However, there are more common instances where we may be asked to do something, or have knowledge that others intend to do or have done something which offends our moral values and sense of right and wrong. Such situations might involve lying on behalf of a colleague or boss, discovering a colleague fiddling their expenses, or knowingly engaging in practices which endanger the health of other workers or customers.

Whether or not the individual decides to compromise his values and go along with such behaviour depends upon:

1. his assessment of his own level of personal responsibility; the classic 'I had no choice, I was only obeying orders' syndrome
2. his estimation of the potential harm as opposed to the benefits of such action. For example, 'If I lie on behalf of my boss, I will feel really bad and it is likely that I will be asked to tell more serious lies in the future' versus 'If I lie on behalf of my boss, nothing really awful

will happen and he will act favourably towards me in the future'

3. the expectation of discovery and punishment

In an organizational setting, because there is greater anonymity and the risks and consequences attached to any action are often less immediate, more diffuse and indirect, moral boundaries are less clear-cut and more fuzzy. Consequently, individuals are more likely to adopt double standards and to behave in ways that they would never consider right and proper in the conduct of their personal lives.

Research has consistently demonstrated that individuals behave differently when in a group or organizational situation. Compared with individuals working alone, groups are more likely to make more risky and extreme decisions. The pressure on the individual to yield and conform to the majority view is often considerable, particularly if the other group members are of a higher status in the organization. As has been discussed, responsibility for action is more diffused in a group, and the sense of personal responsibility is reduced.

Moral or ethical dilemmas in the workplace are particularly problematic and potentially stressful. In such a situation, the individual is likely to feel as if he is between a rock and a hard place. If he decides to turn a blind eye or go along with the situation, the resultant incongruence between personal and organizational values is likely to cause distress. The alternative is also distressing, in that any decision to challenge the behaviour may result in job loss or amount to career suicide.

Richard Nielsen (Nielsen, 1987), a US professor of management, suggests that there are a number of possible courses of action which managers can adopt in such situations:

1. Don't think about it
2. Go along and get along
3. Protest
4. Conscientiously object

5. Leave
6. Secretly blow the whistle (leak documents, write anonymously to superiors, etc.)
7. Publicly blow the whistle
8. Secretly threaten to blow the whistle
9. Engage in sabotage
10. Negotiate and build consensus for change

These strategies vary in terms of the degree to which they are likely to be effective and the amount of personal risk involved.

Don't think/go along

Obviously, such strategies do nothing to stop unethical behaviour in the workplace and are more likely to promote its further continuance. In the short term, the individual may be able to switch off or rationalize his behaviour, but there may be detrimental psychological consequences in the longer term. Behaving unethically or passively condoning such behaviour may ultimately result in dismissal or legal action, as in the case of the *Daily Mirror* board directors, who now face being sued by the Maxwell pension fund holders.

Protect/conscientiously object

Depending on the seriousness and scale of the situation, speaking out and letting people know how you feel may make the individual feel good and is preferable to keeping quiet and bottling things up. But protests of outrage and indignation alone may simply be disregarded or amount to career suicide. A quiet word in the ear of a colleague who is fiddling his expenses may be sufficient to cause him to rethink his behaviour. However, the sole voice of a more junior employee attacking major corporate policies or aspects of organizational behaviour is unlikely to gain a serious or sympathetic hearing and carries considerable personal risk.

Leave

Leaving represents the ultimate protest. Few people can afford, financially or psychologically, or have the moral courage to perform the heroic act of resigning on a matter of principle. Furthermore, leaving the organization is unlikely to cause it to change its behaviour.

Blow the whistle

Any decision to secretly blow the whistle has the advantage over doing so publicly of a reduced fear of retaliation. Although certainly such action will precipitate some form of internal enquiry or witch-hunt. Secretly blowing the whistle has the disadvantage that it often makes the individual feel sneaky, and he then lives in perpetual fear that he will be found out. The same applies to acts of sabotage. Going public is likely to have the most impact. However, in order to do so the individual may firstly have to leave the organization. Before doing this, the individual should also seek legal advice to ascertain whether he is likely to be in breach of any employment contract.

According to Richard Nielsen, secretly threatening to blow the whistle is often the more effective strategy. It has the advantage of giving the individual/organization time to reconsider and change the behaviour. It is also less risky and if it works successfully is unlikely to result in retaliation or any self-recrimination.

Negotiate and build consensus for change

This is different from protesting and objecting in that the individual seeks to confront the unethical behaviour, but at the same time offers a solution or alternative course of action. For example, if a colleague is resorting to fiddling his expenses this may be because (a) he is underpaid, (b) he has large debts, or (c) he thinks it is legitimate to make a little bit extra out of his employer (i.e. everybody is at it!). Depending on the circumstances, it may therefore be appropriate to suggest that (a) he speaks to his boss, (b) he seeks financial advice and support, or (c) this is not the case and what would happen if everybody did the same? Alternatively, work towards introducing more stringent controls and procedures.

Choosing the right course of action

Negotiation and building consensus for change is a strategy which is likely to be effective, and at the same time offers the least personal risk to the individual. However, there are circumstances in which negotiation may fail. In any ethical dilemma, it is important to work through internal channels first before going public. Any complaints should be based on documented evidence and not rumour or hearsay, and should be put in writing whenever possible. In addition, whistle-blowers should try to get the support of other colleagues or union representatives.

It is also important not only for the individual to stay on his best work behaviour, but also to make sure that his information is correct and appropriately presented. Before making any formal complaint or report, it is advisable to speak informally with a senior colleague whom the individual trusts. Such dialogues can help clarify issues. On points of major policy, for example environmental issues, the individual may be unable to change organizational thinking overnight, but directing energy into local action groups may both salve individual consciences and ultimately bring about a change.

Coping With Middle Age: Facing Milestones

Age is something which tends to creep up on us. Suddenly, we reach a point in our lives when we realize that 'old' is no longer a label we only apply to others around us, but is now also applicable to ourselves. Apart from the obvious physical signs of ageing, there are certain life events which psychologically remind us of our mortality (e.g. the loss of our parents, the death of a member of our peer group, the birth of a grandchild, an invitation to join a pre-retirement course).

According to psychologist Donald Super, there are four

broad age-related career stages. The first stage, *exploration*, typically occurs between the ages of 15 and 24, when the individual forms ideas about himself and the world of work, explores opportunities and makes choices as to the type of career and organization to which he is most suited. From the mid-twenties to the early forties, the individual is in the second stage, *establishment*. This stage represents a period when the need to achieve and prove oneself is often very strong. During this period, the individual is typically concerned with directing his energies towards establishing himself in his career and climbing the greasy pole. It is also a time when many individuals are coping with the financial and emotional demands of raising a family and establishing themselves in society more generally. From the mid-forties until retirement, the *maintenance* stage, individuals are more concerned with hanging on and maintaining the position they have achieved, rather than looking for advance further. Earlier career optimism has by now usually been curbed by realism, or possibly pessimism. Finally, the individual enters the fourth stage, which Super terms *decline*. Decline is characterized by a decreasing involvement and participation in work and is typically reached by the age of 65+.

Traditionally, the idea of a mid-life crisis was associated with the age of 40. However, the many youthful examples from the world of showbusiness who have continued to produce popular hit records or remain box-office idols beyond their 40th birthday, coupled with increased life expectancy, have given a certain widespread credibility to the slogan that 'Life begins at 40'. This has arguably had the effect of making the next age milestone (i.e. passing 50) critically more important.

Passing 50 is a significant change for the average male, because that is when the production of the male hormone testosterone begins to decline. From puberty through to middle age, the production of testosterone increases male aggression, competitiveness, self-confidence, self-reliance and assertiveness. Around the age of 50, the male hormone begins a gradual decline, with consequence changes in Boardroom as well as bedroom behaviour.

Most top managers are male, and after 50 is the time for them to enjoy life, to broaden interests and to change pace. But you have to take control. If you are driven, make sure that you are doing the driving rather than the system driving you. You have made a big contribution to your career thus far, so now may be the time to get a better match between what you want and what is needed from you.

The most vulnerable group are executives in their late 40s and 50s, who are also likely to be abusing alcohol and coping with alienated children, ageing parents and extensive financial commitments. But it is still the minority who are damaged by these problems and challenges. If you manage the rest of your career right, and review your management style, then you can cope with the challenges and maintain the excellence of your contribution, along with keeping the buzz in your working life.

Stocktaking at 50

Where are you going to from here? Derek Torrington and Cary Cooper (1990) recommend five options:

> First is **consolidation**, where you settle for doing even better what you are already doing so well. Of all the mountains you have climbed, the one you are at the top of now is where you are going to stop. Instead of looking for new things to do, you find ways of doing the present things better. Let others do the path-breaking, while you concentrate on quality of product, people and performance.

> A second possibility is **transfer**. Try a lateral move, so that you apply your expertise and experience in positions which are different from what you are doing now, but similar. This may be simply a change of colleagues, or it may involve deploying familiar skills in a different way.

This will give you novel challenges and the opportunity to work in different social settings.

Thirdly is **diversification**, where you add variety rather than load to your portfolio. Instead of continuing to try and do everything in your job, you let other people pick up some of the opportunities, while you spend more of your time on management development within the business or on charity work outside it. Your expertise is potentially valuable in all sorts of ways other than making money. Spread it around a little, cast yourself in a different role for a few hours a week. Not only will you enjoy it, and perhaps do some good, you will also learn a lot and get a better perspective on the job you have been doing all your life.

A more radical alternative is **change**, which is a risk because you take up a totally different type of work, like becoming a schoolteacher or training for the priesthood. How is your humility? You will need plenty if you are going to move out of the field in which you have been a success to start afresh as a nonentity. There is always a dash of romance about this sort of bold move, which is often made by those seeking a degree of fulfilment that has hitherto escaped them. Diversification is safer, because you maintain your position and status as an expert at the same time as learning new ways.

The last option, which should be the most logical, but is actually the hardest: *is to step down*. It is crazy that top managers can only move up, and never down the hierarchical pyramid. If you move down, you are stigmatized; there must be something wrong with you. Either you have failed or you are ill. This is less of a problem in other walks of life. In our university, leading academics take it in turn to take on roles like dean, vice principal and head of department. They serve for two or three years and exercise considerable authority before reverting to their traditional academic roles. Lawyers, medical practitioners and actors all expect to change status within their professions at different times of their lives. Managers must soon break the convention that corporate careers are one-way streets, going up or nowhere.

CHAPTER 6

Home and Work

Many of the hassles that people experience in contemporary life stem from the interface between work and home, primarily from the increase in dual-career families, and how this affects roles and relationships at home. In fact, the junior Minister for Social Security, Alistair Burt, MP, in June 1993 indicated as much in a speech about work and the family; 'Too many companies and businesses demand outrageous time commitments from those who work for them, without thought of the damage to family structure or of the strength their employees should get from a sound family life if they are allowed to foster it.' This chapter will explore the changing nature of the family, the difficulties this causes and how individuals might begin to deal with them.

The Changing Nature of Marriage

An interesting way of conceptualizing contemporary marriage has been provided by Charles Handy (1978). He studied husbands and wives in terms of their needs for achievement, dominance, affiliation, and nurturance. As can be seen in Figure 1, he combined achievement and dominance needs and affiliation and nurturance needs, and came up with four patterns which reflect fundamental approaches to life. To arrive at particular marriage patterns, he combined the husbands' orientations which those of the wives.

Although there are 16 possible combinations of marriage patterns, Handy's research turned up only eight patterns, with only four principal patterns occurring. We will look at his four most frequent ones, as shown in Figure 1. The first pattern is of a thrusting husband and a caring wife, which Handy found to be the most frequent pattern and the one which represents the traditional sex-role stereotype. Here the husband is the breadwinner and the wife the home-maker. His goals of success and achievement are her goals as well, and all her efforts are involved in the home and providing him with support, although she is not particularly interested in the details of his work. These marriages are predictable, structured, and create little stress.

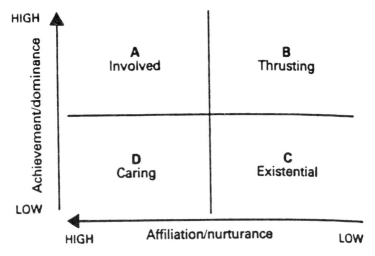

Figure I: Types of Marriages
Source: Handy, 1978

The negative aspects of this pattern are that the wife has difficulty in expressing or meeting her own needs while her children are around. She also may find it difficult to cope when the children leave home or the husband's career reaches its ceiling or, indeed, deteriorates.

The second marriage pattern is the pairing of two thrusters. In this pattern, both the husband and the wife have high needs of achievement and dominance. In the past, the thrusting wife tended to stay at home and either be frustrated at not achieving her own goals, or attempt to meet her achievement needs in homemaking activities. Thrusters usually desire support or the caring role, and if both are making this demand known, considerable discontent can result. This is also the pairing situation most likely to lead to dual-career families, confronting the changing conception of woman's role in the home. Naturally, if both thrusters become thoroughly involved in their worklife, as they are likely to do, their domestic arrangements and circumstances are likely to be very chaotic indeed. Since, by definition, thrusters – whether husband or wife – need the comforts of the home environment, the conflicts, tensions, and stress in the family will be enormous. In addition, these types of relationships become very much more strained when children arrive on the scene because the husband attempts to get his wife to play out the traditional sex-role stereotype (that is, she must give up her job), and draws on the guilt he knows his wife has buried just below the surface of her emancipation.

The third pattern is the partnership of two involved people. Although the husband and wife are both high achievers, with a tendency to be dominant in their interpersonal relationship, they also place a high value on caring and belonging. As Handy suggests, 'they prefer to share arenas, not separate them'. The stress level in these marriages is very high, since both partners have an underlying thrusting instinct, but this is tempered with a caring element that encourages them to confront one another with problems. In contrast, two thrusters would avoid resolution by compromise and discussion, and would seek victory through defeat. Although in this third pattern one partner or the other may have to do something in the short run that he or she would prefer not to, there is sufficient flexibility in the marriage to provide short-term support so that he or she can end up doing what either wants to do in the longer term.

And finally, the last marriage pattern is an involved husband with a caring wife. Here the husband is highly achievement-oriented but also values the caring aspect of relationships. The husband is likely to be under a great deal of stress, since not only is he ambitious, but he also cares about other people and is very concerned not to hurt others.

Because the husband is sensitive to other people's feelings, he feels guilty when his wife commits herself solely to him (although he does want her social support). As Handy suggests, these relationships are 'less predictable and the tensions less well contained. These relationships are more intense and emotional. There is more questioning and more effort to rework roles than in the traditional marriage.'

Different combinations of roles can create problems, as Handy indicates:

1. Where the activity pattern of a marriage fits that which would normally be required by the underlying mix of personalities there will be less familiar stress. For example, if an A-A couple (see Figure 1) are forced by the success of the husband and the needs of the children to adopt a B-D pattern, family stress is likely to be increased.

2. If the pattern of husband-wife relationship doesn't change with changes in the central life interests of each member, there is liable to be more family stress.

3. If there are changes in the activity pattern at home or work which do not fit with one of the satisfactory marriage patterns above, then either the job or the attitudes or the partners must change if stress and conflict are to be avoided.

Dual-Career Marriages

Economic pressures and the needs of women to pursue careers outside the home have led Britain and many other Western countries into being dual-career cultures (Cooper, Cooper & Eaker, 1988). Tim and Francine Hall, in their book, *Two-Career Couples*, suggest that the 'traditional family model of the husband as breadwinner and wife as homemaker, together "till death do us part", is becoming a vestige of a past society'. In the US, fewer than 10% of American families are of the traditional working husband, homemaker wife and two children, and in the UK, while the male labour force has increased by 3% in the last 20 years, the female labour force has grown by over 40%.

Although the dual-career couple can be liberating, it can also create an enormous number of daily hassles for its participants. Like Handy, the Halls contend that the problems associated with two-career families can be great, depending on the nature of the marriage itself. They start defining the two-career couple as 'two people who share a lifestyle that includes (1) cohabitation, (2) separate work roles for both partners, and (3) a love relationship that supports and facilitates both.' They contend that there are four dual-career family role structures: accommodators, adversaries, allies, and acrobats. The **accommodator** pattern usually has 'one partner who is high in career involvement and low in home involvement, while the other partner is high in home involvement and low in career involvement'. The difference between this pattern and the traditional family one is that either gender can play either role. The possible stresses and strains are kept to a minimum. There are an increasing number of men prepared to play the traditional female role, while wives become the breadwinners – although the movement in this direction is insignificant in comparison to the number of families with working husbands and wives.

On the other hand, the **adversaries** are very much the two working thrusters described by Handy, a couple in which 'both partners are highly involved in their careers, and have low involvement in home, family, or partner support roles'. As in the two-thruster marriages, this is the most stressful marital pattern, where there is competition over priorities, avoidance of non-work roles in the family, conflict in terms of career development of either member, and the unwillingness to give up any of their career identity to meet the needs of husband/wife or the family unit (unless the work costs are negligible).

The third type is the **allies** pattern in which 'two people are both highly involved in either career or home and family roles, with little identity tied up in the other'. This is broken down into two different orientations. In the former, neither partner identifies with a career. Both derive their primary satisfaction from their family and their relationship. In the other, they identify strongly with their jobs and not the family, and 'their identities are not tied up in having a well-ordered home, gourmet dinners, entertaining or, often, children. The support structure may be "purchased", in dinners out, maids, and catering services, or simply not exist.' The potential stress problem in the latter case is that the couple don't have the time required to maintain the relationship as a support base for their independent activities.

The fourth type of couple is the **acrobats**. As the name implies, this type of couple is made up of 'partners who are highly involved in all their roles, both work and family'. They perceive the home and work roles as equally important and, therefore, are very vulnerable to overload. As Hall and Hall suggest, their major source of stress derives from the 'conflict of trying to meet all the demands – having a successful career, being a good partner, having a well-ordered home, providing real and emotional support for the spouse, and still finding time for the relationship'.

Coping with Multiple Roles

Throughout the 1990s, the number of dual-career couples continues to grow, but society's expectations concerning family roles still tend to lag behind reality (Lewis & Cooper, 1989). If the activities of dual-career husbands and wives conflict with these expectations, this can cause conflict and guilt. Mothers of young children are particularly vulnerable to feelings of guilt, because they do not conform to society's traditional definition of a good mother. Equally, some men feel that their masculinity is threatened if their powerful position as major breadwinner is challenged. Such problems are less severe for the New Man, but many individuals who articulate non-traditional views of these changing roles have difficulty in completely overcoming the powerful influence of their early socialization. This ambivalence about gender roles underlies problems such as who does what in the home, where the family should locate and commitments to child care.

The male work ethic, which fails to acknowledge the interdependence of work and family, issues of equality and ambivalence about sex roles, complicates the lives of dual-career families. It cannot be denied that a dual-career way of life is very demanding and can be stressful at times, but it is also potentially satisfying and fulfilling.

Most of the research investigating coping strategies of dual-career couples has been based on a model developed by Tim Hall (1972). He described three approaches to coping with multiple roles, summarized by Sue Lewis and Cary Cooper in their book, *Career Couples*:

Type 1 coping: structure role redefinition

This is an attempt to alter other people's expectations of a particular role. For instance, a wife may renegotiate with her husband the expectation that she should be responsible for all domestic work, or an employee may negotiate with his or her boss about what should be expected in a particular job. Type 1 strategies include delegation and refusing to take on extra work.

Type 2 coping: personal role definition

This is an attempt by an individual to change his or her own self-expectations and behaviours, without necessarily trying to alter other people's attitudes. Making a personal decision to limit activities in the career, spouse or parental roles would be examples of Type 2 coping. Strategies include eliminating roles, for example, giving up voluntary work or union activity, restricting social contacts and establishing priorities.

Type 3 coping: reactive role behaviour or role expansion

Instead of attempting to change the situation or alter self-expectations, an individual may attempt to organize himself or herself in such a way that all role demands can be met. For instance, an overworked mother may work even harder to fit the superwoman image rather than delegating more domestic work to her husband, reducing work involvement or lowering standards in the home. Strategies which enable individuals to do all this include planning, scheduling, working harder and denying that a situation is stressful.

Types 1 and 2 coping are both active coping orientations, in that they involve redefining roles in an attempt to make the situation more manageable. Type 3 coping or role expansion is more passive. It involves an acceptance of all role demands. Attempts are made to satisfy everyone's expectations by being more organized or by using techniques which will minimize the subsequent stress without eliminating or reducing its cause.

Since role and overload problems tend to be greater for women, it is not surprising that the majority of research into the effectiveness of these strategies has examined the coping behaviour of employed mothers. As Lewis and Cooper (1989) highlight, there is evidence that role redefinition (Types 1 and 2 coping) tends to be more stressful, producing high levels of career satisfaction, and to be more successful than role expansion in reducing conflicts between work and home (Beutell & Greenhaus, 1983). Nevertheless, different approaches, they suggest, tend to be used in relation to different situations. Active role redefinition strategies are perceived as more effective in dealing with work-related problems (Alpert & Culbertson, 1987), but mothers are generally reluctant to redefine expectations concerning the parental role. In addition, women who have traditional attitudes are more likely to try to fit everything in than nontraditional women, who are better able to consider ways of adapting their role. Furthermore, although role redefinition strategies appear to be more effective overall, there is some evidence that they are less effective for professional women with young children, because of internal guilt feelings (Gilbert, Holohan & Manning, 1981). Underlying traditional attitudes towards motherhood make it very difficult for women, even those who articulate non-traditional beliefs, to alter their own or other people's expectations of the role of good mother. Therefore, active coping strategies which aim to change people's expectations associated with specific roles are most effective, but women's early childhood experiences often prevent these techniques from being successful, because traditional attitudes to the maternal role elicit feelings of guilt.

Reducing the Working Family Tensions

In addition to dealing with the role problem in dual-career relationships, couples need to find specific techniques to reduce tension in order to more adequately consider the deeper-level issues. Bebe Campbell-Moore, in her book, *Successful Women: Angry Men*, suggests a series of steps in lowering the temperature when inevitable conflicts occur:

1. Find time to talk in a relaxed way. This may involve deliberate setting aside some time from busy schedules when lack of interruptions is guaranteed.
2. Learn techniques of effective communication. Using the wrong words can alienate. It is better to take responsibility for your own feelings and behaviour than to accuse. For example, say 'I feel you could do more in the house' rather than 'You never do enough in the house'. Your feelings can be discussed, but an accusation merely makes the other person defensive.
3. Listen to what the other person says. It is useful to reflect back, to show that you have really heard and accept his or her feelings. For example, 'It sounds as though you feel really angry with me. Can you tell me what it is that I do which makes you feel that way?'

If problems have become really overwhelming:

4. It might help to agree an official time-out or call a temporary truce. A temporary separation, such as separate holidays, may provide time to work out a solution.

5. Don't try to solve all problems at once. Work on one at a time.
6. If necessary, elicit the help of a professional counsel-lor.

Murray Watts and Cary Cooper, in their book. *Relax*, also come up with several suggestions of dealing with marital problems when one if not both partners are showing signs of stress:

- People under severe stress lose their perspective. Try to keep yours.
- Don't let the stress infect you, making you anxious. The problems will get much worse if you add to them. Use mental and physical relaxation exercises. Find space and time to be alone.
- Don't get drawn into endless rows. Your anger will serve to justify the anger of the other person, which needs exposing as a problem.
- Be kind to yourself. Don't be a martyr. The carer needs caring for too. Make sure you have at least one person you can off-load your problems on to. Express your anger and frustrations to them. Clear the air regularly.
- Look for early-warning signs of stress in those you love. Choose a moment when your partner or relative is calm and relaxed. Gently point out your concern to him, without any accusation. 'I'm worried about you. You're smoking a lot more than you used to. You must feel under a lot of strain.'
- Take action on his behalf in cases where his will is para-lysed. 'I think we should talk about your depression to our doctor. Let me make an appointment. I'll come with you.'
- When resistance to any change is put up over a long period, be firm. You cannot go on listening to the same gripes and moans thousands of times without your re-lationship deteriorating. Be loving but make it clear that you are not only a son, daughter, wife, but a person in

your own right with your own needs. You need them to find a way through.

- Be a sounding-board but not a duckboard. If your feelings are being ignored and you are being trodden down, insist on some time away, a day, a weekend, with friends or alone. Keep renewing your strength.
- Don't be a co-dependent, worsening the stressed person's problems by your need to care for him. Don't hold back his progress by indulging his – because it makes you feel needed. His self-destructive attitudes or behaviour can never be the foundation for a healthy relationship.
- Be an enabler. See yourself as the one who helps the sufferer to help himself.
- Help him to focus on the present and the future. To talk about what can be done, not what cannot be undone.
- Try making a list of problem areas in his life. Do it together. Look at some options.
- Believe that things can change, without being unsympathetic or glib. Be the eyes of the sufferer when he can't see beyond his problems. Remind him that this is temporary. He will see clearly and hope again.

Managing Time Out

Another way in which couples can begin to cope with the pressures of everyday life is to create time-out periods in the year. It has been recently reported in the *Daily Express* that GPs are prescribing holiday brochures rather than pills for many of their hassled patients. In a survey, 83% of GPs believed patients who took regular holidays had fewer stress problems, in spite of the fact that working people in Britain have fewer national holidays than their European counterpart: UK 33 days a year, compared to 41 for Germany, 36 for Italy and 34 for France.

Managing time out means creating time and space for you

and your partner, and in some cases the children as well. Instead of people polluting the beaches of Spain or Portugal during the summer, perhaps dual-career couples ought to take frequent but short time-outs during the course of a stressful work year. There are a range of possible time-outs, each of which might serve a different function:

Time out with partner
When the signs are present that things are not right in the relationship (e.g. lack of any communication, constant avoidance activity like obsession with TV, increased irritability, etc.), it is time to get away together. Get someone to look after the kids, cats, plants, etc. and take a long weekend. Get away and allow yourselves some space and time to talk, to *be* with one another, to begin to open up.

Time out with family
The hassles of dual-career couples also adversely affect children, and occasionally it is necessary for whole families to take time out, whether by short holidays or long weekends away. Distress of children of working parents doesn't always manifest itself in an obvious way, but the symptoms are real and should be attended to, as this comment from an executive women illustrates:

> My eldest boy is 14, he's such an uncommunicative character; communications happen, but in grunts and sudden rushes of confidential information, and then silences that to on for days. He might suddenly show quite a warmth towards me when I come back from a business trip, which happens quite regularly. It seems to me to indicate that he has in some vague way been disturbed by my absence and is glad to see me back, even though he wouldn't like to say so.

Relocations

Another problematic home-work interface event is job relocation. The labour force in the UK and in Europe generally is becoming much more mobile, which is particularly the case for managers and other professionals. Indeed, it is now estimated that United Kingdom managers change jobs about once every three years. Research in North America and other Western countries suggests that managerial mobility there is increasing even more rapidly. But relocation, although more frequent among middle-class/white-collar workers, does not affect them alone. With the decline in the economy in the last couple of years, and the increase in blue-collar unemployment, workers in the mining and steel industries have been encouraged to up sticks and leave their home towns for greener pastures.

Whatever the background one comes from, moving can be a traumatic and stressful event, depending on two factors. The first involves the situation in which the individual is involved, or his or her life area, such as job, family, and outside activities. The second factor involves characteristics of the individual – age, qualification, job skills and personality, that is, the base from which he or she views and interprets the world. These stresses are highlighted by the wife of a bank manager who had finally been forced to relocate:

What is often not realized by the bank is the tremendous burden moving house places on the wife. Buying and selling houses is very time-consuming, the average length of time for our moves being about six months. A promotion move occurs at any time; it may be a difficult time in the school year for children, the housing market may be awkward, the list is endless, but the bank takes very little account of any of the problems, and it is generally the wife who has the responsibility of sorting out the difficulties. The bank's attitude is that wives like new carpets and curtains, therefore they enjoy moving house! This really annoys me – generalizing about women. Bank wives are not expected to think, just to accept! We are supposed to conform to a set model – that of the perfect housewife, ready to comply to the demands of a husband's career, to enjoy homemaking but not to get so attached to our homes that we object to giving them up, to be totally

dependent on our husbands, both financially and emotionally, yet capable of living apart for long periods, with
the added ability of being a financial and legal organizer
of the complexities and difficulties which surround buying
and selling homes in two different parts of the country.
The stereotype role of the bank wife is full of contradictions.

It is not only the difficulties which surround the operation of buying and selling houses which bank wives have
to cope with. The financial rewards of a promotion are
negligible and often, the first twelve months after a house
move, people are financially worse off than before promotion. Also a promotion carries exactly the same salary
rise whether it involves a house move or not, so you don't
even have the dubious consolation of a higher income to
make up for all the disruptions and upsets to family life a
house move can incur.

Cary Cooper and Judi Marshall (1979) carried out a study
which explored the stresses and strains of job transfer on
middle and senior executives in the United Kingdom. This
study can help illustrate some of the problems for the individual relocating at different stages in life.

For instance, *younger single men* in the sample reported
problems such as the pressure of starting a new job at a critical and closely watched phase in their career; the culture
shock of starting work after life at university; having no
separate world to retire to in the evenings to help switch off;
the problems of house-hunting; being lonely in a strange
town often populated by contented married couples; leaving
friends behind and trying to maintain contacts, perhaps with
a possible future wife.

For *young marrieds*, it appeared that most couples felt
free and willing to meet the challenge of a new community;
it is typically at this time that they have most friends and
activities outside the home. Their lack of constraints makes
it easier to follow one or the other's career, to be more
mobile. In a dual-career marriage, complications arise: is

one partner to sacrifice his or her career for the promotional move of the other? How does the partner find another rewarding occupation after the move? If both have a busy career, how do they manage the complexities of finding a new home and moving, and are they able, in their limited spare time, to form new social relationships?

For *married couples with a young family*, the problems of relocation are complex, both for the more traditional marriage, where the wife is at home, and for the dual-career family. For the latter, house-hunting becomes a major problem, both because the wife is too tied down to participate much, and because house choice becomes more crucial and the criteria more exacting. Size and nearness to schools and shops become important and, for the housebound wife, potential friends must also be considered. Separation is an emotionally draining time for all the family. If the wife is at home, her adaption to and happiness in her new environment become critical factors. The couple may find it harder to make out-of-work friends, tied down as they are, and place more emphasis on nearness (the neighbours) and same-boat acquaintances (couples with children of the same age and interests). They must find new social support systems, and new child and home help if they both work.

The children, as Ivancevich and Matteson (1980) suggest, are also affected by the move:

> certain age groups are more susceptible to relocation stress. Pre-schoolers experience feelings of loss and insecurity. They may even interpret a relocation as a form of punishment. A young child may revert to infantile behaviour such as thumb-sucking or bed-wetting, or they may experience more nightmares. Children in grade school may experience similar feelings of insecurity. Teenagers, to whom peer approval and relationships are so important, frequently have a particularly difficult time.

Relocation is, therefore, an extremely stressful event at this stage.

Empty nesters, many of whom are still moving at this

stage of life, may have come to regard mobility as an acceptable way of life. Others, though, express concern that they never settle down anywhere, and that they are not providing a stable home for their children and grandchildren to visit. Choosing retirement sites becomes a problem for those who have lived in so many places and belonged to none.

Relocation is a recurring problem, often inducing stress among a number of family members. In the 1990s and beyond, with more women pursuing careers, the prospects of professional men or women being available for rapid deployment will substantially decrease. This will create a number of stressful choices for the partner in terms of the direction and the security of his or her career.

Relocation: exploring possibilities and alternatives

As Lewis and Cooper (1989) suggest, it is often necessary for married couples faced with the prospect of the relocation of one spouse to deviate from accepted norms of behaviour. The traditional pattern is for the wife to move with her husband's job, whilst the husband moving with his wife's job is unconventional. There are various strategies between these two extremes. Making your position clear from the outset may be one way of anticipating and avoiding future dilemmas. Lewis and Cooper suggest a range of positions which can be stated clearly upon taking up employment.

1. Make it clear that you will not be willing to relocate.
2. Make it clear that you will not be willing to relocate unless a suitable position is also found for your spouse.
3. Make it clear from the outset that you are willing to relocate and that your family poses no obstacle. This may be particularly necessary for married women who may be passed over for promotion on the assumption that they cannot be mobile.
4. State that requests for relocation will be considered in the light of circumstances at the time, including your spouse's career situation, children's schooling and so on.

At a later stage dilemmas may still arise. If so, Lewis and Cooper feel you should consider the following alternatives.

1. Refuse to relocate. This may involve loss of promotion and will reflect your life priorities.
2. If the new location is not too geographically distant, consider moving so that both of you can travel to work from one home which is approximately equidistant from your work locations. This may involve substantial travelling time.
3. Consider alternating decisions in each partners favour. A move can be made now to facilitate one person's career on the understanding that the next move will favour the other spouse.
4. Consider living apart during the week or for longer periods.
5. Consider other creative solutions. Mary Maples (1981) suggests that one solution may be for one partner to take up flying as a hobby!

If you are faced with a relocation dilemma, it may be useful to list these and any other strategies you can think of, and write down what might be the advantages and disadvantages of each one. Any decision will involve some sacrifice, in terms of career prospects, family life or travelling time. Your final decision will depend upon where you priorities lie in terms of your life values.

How Organizations Can Help Working Parents

Until recently, few employers did much to help working women with children to juggle the demands of job and family. Some companies developed job-sharing and part-time work schemes. But many of these were limited to jobs of low status, with restricted access to training and few opportunities for promotion.

Now, however, as more companies realize the need to re-think their working arrangements for career couples, a number of alternatives are proving their worth, as Lewis and Cooper suggest in *Career Couples*.

V-time
This stands for voluntary reduced time – a system that allows full-time employees to reduce working hours for a specified period with a reduction in salary. It differs from the usual concept of part-time work in that it is temporary, with a return to full-time work guaranteed.

All employee benefits are maintained, although they may be altered to a pro-rata basis. Usually the schedule remains in force for an agreed period, perhaps 6 to 12 months, to allow employees and employers to try it out, with an assurance that the commitment can be renegotiated or terminated.

The time off may be taken by working shorter days or weeks' or a block of time may be taken, perhaps during school holidays. The Alliance & Leicester Building Society has introduced a pilot scheme that allows time off during the holidays for those with children between 5 and 14. V-time may also be used for gaining new skills or responding to a health problem.

Career-break schemes
Fewer than 7% of women in the UK return to full-time work immediately after maternity leave, but 90% return after a longer break.

Some organizations, recognizing that many women prefer to spend more time with their infants than maternity leave allows, have taken steps to provide longer career breaks. Re-entry and retainer schemes have been initiated (e.g. by NatWest Bank, Barclays, ICL) to allow women to interrupt their usual work for a number of years, after which they can return with no loss of seniority.

The employee is usually expected to undertake at least two weeks' paid relief work for the company during each year of her absence, and is provided with regular information packs, as well as a refresher course on her return. In practice, many work for more than two weeks a year.

The scheme may permit one five-year break or two shorter breaks, each dating from the end of statutory maternity leave. Many women prefer the two breaks, which enable them to return to work between the births of a first and second child.

Career breaks are open, in principle, to men as well as women, although in practice they tend to be taken only by women. Organizations permitting two short breaks could encourage their being shared between the two parents.

The benefits of a career-break scheme are becoming increasingly apparent. For example:

- They ensure that participants remain in touch with their work, maintaining confidence, expertise and knowledge.
- Firms offering career breaks will attract young women with talent and ambition, because they will have less fear of having to choose between family and career.
- They ensure investment in training is not lost, and after a break a minimum of retraining is required.
- They provide role models of women successfully combining career and family.
- They improve motivation, time-keeping and productivity.
- They increase flexibility by providing a pool of trained staff to draw on when people are absent, or during peak periods.
- They reduce stress among new mothers and fathers.

The career-break scheme first introduced by NatWest has served as a model for many forward-looking organizations and professional bodies that are now adopting similar schemes. The Law Society suggests that those operating such a scheme should ensure maximum benefit by advertising themselves as a career-break employer, in much the same way as many organizations claim to be equal-opportunity employers.

Sabbaticals

In Sweden, the idea of up to a year off, after a certain period of work, has been institutionalized in a wide range of occupations. In the UK, six-month sabbaticals for employees aged 50 or over with at least 25 years' service have been introduced by the John Lewis group to allow employees to do things they enjoy which would not otherwise be possible.

Sabbaticals are available at all levels. People in specialist and senior management posts are encouraged not to feel indispensable, although they are required to give longer notice than other employees. Arrangements are made to cover their absences by creating an opportunity for a trainee, or reorganizing colleagues' responsibilities to share out the work.

This provides opportunities for employees to take on new responsibilities, which can contribute to personal and career development. Colleagues are willing to co-operate, knowing that they, too, will have the opportunity of a sabbatical.

Clearly, the age requirement in this particular scheme rules it out for new parents, but sabbaticals may be used to fulfil other family obligations that occur at a later stage. Apart from the care of sick relatives, people might wish to spend their time visiting adult children living abroad. But the fact that the system works well has implications for the organization of leave of absence for younger employees, especially for those taking maternity or paternity leave.

Men as well as women can benefit from policies that aim to ease the transition to parenthood. Just as women need role models who successfully combine career and motherhood, men need role models of fathers willing to accommodate their career for child care.

Organizations can play a part in bringing about a change in attitudes. They can encourage fathers who show an interest in paternity leave or career breaks by guaranteeing that their career prospects will not be harmed. Ultimately, the most helpful organizations will be those offering the most choices to new parents so that they can suit their needs.

The 1980s was the era of the entrepreneurial and thrusting organization, the 1990s is likely to be one of corporate and community responsibility for the family, as Alistair Burt, junior Minister of Social Security, suggests: 'The success of the 1980s in Conservative political terms was to re-state the role of the individual in society, and in that classic phrase "roll back the frontiers of the state" in so many different ways. But whilst this was a success in economic terms, it left a gap in our thinking in the development of social policy. There is such a thing as society, and it stands or falls on the strength of the individuals who make it up. The 1980s was all about empowering the individual, but what we have to do in the 1990s is seek to marry such empowerment with a community structure which makes use of it.'

References

Chapter 1 – Stress is a Four-Letter Word: What it means and what it costs

Albrecht, K. (1979). *Stress and the Manager. Making It work For You.* New Jersey: Prentice-Hall.

Basowitz, H., Persky, H., Karchin, S.J. & Grinker, R.R. (1955). *Anxiety and Stress.* New York: McGraw Hill.

Breslow, L. & Buell, P. (1975). 'Mortality from coronary heart disease and physical activity of work in California'. *Journal of Chronic Diseases*, *11*, 615-25.

Buck, V. (1972). *Working Under Pressure.* London: Staples Press.

Carruthers, M.E. (1976). Risk factor control. Paper presented to the conference entitled 'Stress of Air-Traffic Control Office', Manchester, April.

Cobb, S. & Rose, R.H. (1973). 'Hypertension, peptic ulcer and diabetes in air-traffic controllers'. *Journal of the Australian Medical Association*, *224*, 489-92.

Coch, L. & French, J.R.P. (1948). 'Overcoming resistance to change'. *Human Relations*, *1*, 512-32.

Cooper, C.L. (1984). 'Executive stress: A ten-country comparison'. *Human Relations*, *1*, 395-407.

Cooper, C.L., Cooper, R.D. & Eaker, L.H. (1988). *Living with Stress.* London: Penguin Books.

Cooper, C.L. & Smith, M.J. (1985). *Job Stress and Blue-Collar Work.* London and New York: John Wiley & Sons.

Cox, T. (1978). *Stress.* London: Macmillan.

Cummings, T. & Cooper, C.L. (1979). 'A cybernetic frame-work for the study of occupational stress'. *Human Relations, 32,* 395-419.

Dale, B. & Cooper, C.L. (1992). *Total Quality and Human Resources.* Oxford: Blackwell Publishers.

Earnshaw, J. & Cooper, C.L. (1991). 'Worker's compensation in stress-related claims'. *Work and Stress,* 5 (2), 253-8.

French, J.R.P. & Caplan, R.D. (1972). In A.J. Marrow (ed.), *The Failure of Success.* New York: Amacon, 31-66.

Hinkle, L.E. (1973). 'The concept of stress in the biological social sciences'. *Stress Medicine and Man, 1,* 31-48.

Ivancevich, J.M. & Matteson, M.T. (1980). *Stress and Work.* Illinois: Scott, Foresman & Co.

Ivancevich, J.M., Matteson, M.T. & Richards, E.P. (1985). 'Who's liable for stress at work'. *Harvard Business Review,* March-April.

Lazarus, R.S. (1976). *Patterns of Adjustment.* New York: McGraw-Hill.

Margolis, B., Kroes, W. & Quinn, R. (1974).'Job stress: An unlisted occupational hazard'. *Journal of Occupational Medicine, 16* (10), 654-61.

Melhuish, A. (1978). *Executive Health.* London: Business Books.

Pincherle, A. (1972). 'Fitness for work'. *Proceedings of the Royal Society of Medicine, 65,* 321-4.

Quick, J.C. & Quick, J.D. (1984). *Organizational Stress and Preventive Management.* New York: McGraw-Hill.

Russek, H.I. & Zohman, B.L. (1958). 'Relative significance of heredity, diet and occupational stress in CHD of young adults'. *American Journal of Medical Sciences, 235,* 266-75.

Sauter, S.L., Hurrell, J.J. & Cooper, C.L. (1989). *Job Control and Worker Health.* Chichester & New York: John Wiley & Sons.

Selye, H. (1946). 'The General Adaptation Syndrome and the disease of adaptation'. *Journal of Clinical Endocrinology, 6,* 117.

Chapter 2 – Managing Your Desk

Adair, J. (1982). *Effective Time Management*. London: Pan Books.

Akersted, T. (1985). 'Shifted sleep hours'. *Annals of Clinical Research*, 27 (5), 273-9.

Aronson, E. et al (1966) cited in Gross, R.D. (1987). *Psychology: The Science of Mind and Behaviour*. London: Edward Arnold.

Beals, C., Hopson, B. & Scally, M. (1991). *Assertiveness: A Positive Process*. London: Mercury Business Paperbacks.

Bradley, G. (1983). 'Effects of computerization on work environment and health from the perspective of equality between sexes'. *Occupational Health Nursing*, 31, 35-9.

Breslow, L. & Buell, P. (1975). Mortality from coronary heart disease and physical activity of work in California. *Journal of Chronic Diseases*, 11, 615-25.

Cartwright, S., Cooper, C.L. & Barron, A. (1993). 'Manager stress and road accidents'. *Journal of General Management*, in press.

Coopers & Lybrand (1993). *Working with VDUs*.

Froggatt, H. & Stamp, P. (1991). *Managing Pressure at Work*. London: BBC Books.

Harris, T.A. (1969). *I'm Okay – You're Okay: A Practical Guide to Transactional Analysis*. New York: Harper and Row.

Johannson, G. & Aronsson, G. (1984). 'Stress reactions in computerized administrative work'. *Journal of Organizational Behavior*, 5, 159-81.

Liff, S. (1990). 'Clerical workers and information technology: gender relations and occupational change'. *New Technology, Work and Employment*, 5 (1), 44-45.

Oldham, G.R. (1985). 'Effects of changes in workspace partitions and spatial density of employee reactions: A quasi-experiment'. *Journal of Applied Psychology*, 73, 253-8.

Rubin, Z. & McNeil, E.B. (3rd Ed., 1983). *The Psychology of Being Human*. London: Harper and Row. Chapter 4.

Townend, A. (1991). *Developing Assertiveness*. London: Routledge.

Wallas, G. (1926). 'The art of thought'. In Vernon, P.E. (ed.). (1970) *Creativity*. Harmondsworth: Penguin.

Chapter 3 – Dealing with Difficult People at Work

Caplan, R.D., Cobb, S., French, J.R.P., Van Harrison, R. & Pinneau, S.R. (1975). *Job Demands and Worker Health: Main Effects and Occupational Differences*. NIOSH Research Report, Cincinnati, Ohio.

Cooper, C.L. & Payne, R. (1988). *Cause, Coping and Consequences of Stress at Work*. Chichester: John Wiley & Sons.

Cox, C. & Cooper, C.L. (1988). *High Fliers: An Anatomy of Managerial Success*. Oxford & New York: Blackwell.

Heller, J. (1975). *Something Happened*. New York: Ballantine Books.

Lazarus, R.S. (1966). *Psychological Stress & Coping Process*. New York: McGraw-Hill.

Makin, P., Cooper C.L. & Cox, C. (1988). *Managing People at Work*. London: Routledge.

McClelland, D.C. (1961). *The Achieving Society*. Princeton, N.J: Van Nostrand.

McClelland, D.C. (1965). 'Achieving motivation can be developed'. *Harvard Business Review*, November.

Quick, J.C. & Quick, J.D. (1984). *Organizational Stress and Preventive Management*. New York: McGraw-Hill.

Watts, M. & Cooper, C.L. (1992). *Relax: Dealing with Stress*. London: BBC Books.

Chapter 4 – Coping with Culture

Berne, E. (1964). *Games People Play*. New York: Grove Press.

Bransford, J., & Johnson, M. (1973). 'Consideration of some problems of comprehension' in Chase, W.D. (ed.) *Visual and Information Processing*, New York: Academic Press.

Cooper, C.L. (1991). 'The Meeting'. *The Independent on Sunday*, 10 June.

Cox, M. & Cox, C. (1980). 'Ten years of transactional analysis'. In Beck, J. & Cox. C. (eds.). *Advances in Management Education*. New York: John Wiley & Sons.

Harrison, R. (1972). 'Understanding your organization's character'. *Harvard Business Review, 50* (23), 119-28.

Harrison, R. (1987). *Organizational Culture and Quality of Service: A Strategy for Releasing Love in the Workplace*. London: Association for Management Education and Development. Chapter 4.

Skov, D., Valbjorn, O. & Pederson, B.V. (1989). 'Influence of personal characteristics, job-related factors and psychosocial factors on the sick building syndrome'. *Journal of Work Environment, 15*, 286-95.

Chapter 5 – Unexpected Workplace Events

Alfred Marks Bureau. (1982). *Sex in the Office*. London: Alfred Marks Bureau

Altendorf, D.M. (1986). 'When cultures clash: a case study of the Texaco takeover of Getty Oil and the impact of acculturation on the acquired firm;. Ph.D. dissertation, Graduate School of Business Administration, University of Southern California.

Bart, P.B. (1981) 'A study of woman who were raped and avoided rape'. Journal of Social Issues, 37, 123-137.

Burke, T., Maddock, S. & Rose, A. (1993). 'How ethical is British business? Research Working Paper Series 2, No. 1. University of Westminster, Faculty of Business Management & Social Studies.

Cartwright, S. & Cooper, C.L. (1989). 'Predicting success in joint venture organizations in information technology – a cultural perspective'. *Journal of General Management, 15*, 39-52.

Cartwright, S. & Cooper, C.L. (1992). *Mergers and Acquisitions : The Human Factor*. Oxford: Butterworth Heinemann.

References

Cohen, L.R. (1983). 'Nonverbal (mis)communication between managerial men and women'. *Business Horizons, 26* (1), 13-17.

Colatosi, C. & Karg, E. (1992). *Stopping Sexual Harassment: A Handbook for Union and Workplace Activists.* Detroit: Labor Education and Research Project.

Crull, P. (1982). 'Stress effects of sexual harassment on the job: Implications for counseling'. *American Journal of Orthopsychiatry, 52,* 539-44.

Eggert, M. (1991). *Outplacement: A Guide to Management and Delivery.* London: Institute of Personnel Management.

Equal Opportunities Working Party (1981). *Report on Sexual Harassment.* Liverpool: NALGO.

Equal Opportunities Commission (1983). *Sexual Harassment of Women at Work: A Study from West Yorkshire.*

Gutek, B.A. (1985). *Sex and the Workplace.* San Francisco: Jossey-Bass.

Holmes, T. & Cartwright, S. (1993). Career change post-35: myth or reality?' *Employee Relations,* in press.

Holmes, T.H. & Rahe, R.H. (1967). 'The social readjustment rating scale'. *Journal of Psychosomatic Research, 11,* 213-18.

Hopson, B. & Scally, M. (1984). *'Build Your Own Rainbow'* Leeds: Lifeskill Associates.

Ivancevich, J.M., Schweiger, D.M. & Power, F.R. (1987). 'Strategies for managing human resource issues during mergers and acquisitions'. *Human Resource Planning, 12* (1), 19-35.

Jensen, I.W. & Gutek, B. A. (1983). Attributions and assignment of responsibility in sexual harassment. *Journal of Social Issues* 38 (4) 121-136.

Kasinky, R.G., cited in Colatosi, C. & Karg, E. (1992). *Stopping Sexual Harassment: A Handbook for Union and Workplace Activists.* Detroit: Labor Education and Research Project.

Medea, A. & Thompson, K. (1874). *Against Rape.* New York: Farrar, Strauss & Giroux.

Mirvis, P.H. (1985). 'Negotiations after the sale: the roots and ramifications of conflict in an acquisition'. *Journal of Organizational Behavior*, 6(1), 65-84.

NAS/UWT (1987). Unpublished preliminary report by NAS/UWT on results of sexual harassment survey carried out in Birmingham schools. Cited in Rubenstein, M. (1988). *The Dignity of Women at Work*. Luxembourg: Office for Official Publications of the European Communities.

Nelson, A. & Cooper, C.L. (1993). 'The impact of privatization on employee job satisfaction and wellbeing'. *Journal of Occupational and Organizational Psychology*, submitted.

Nelson-Bolles, R. (1989). *What Color is Your Parachute?* New York: Ten Speed Press.

Nielsen, R. (1987). 'What can managers do about unethical management?' *Journal of Business Ethics*, 6 (4), 309-20.

Phillips, C.M., Stockdale, J.E. & Joeman, L.M. (1989). *The Risks in Going to Work, the Nature of People's Work, the Risks they Encounter and the Incidence of Sexual Harassment, Physical Attack and Threatening Behaviour*. London: The Suzy Lamplugh Trust.

Popovich, P.M. & Licata, B.J. (1987). 'A role model approach to sexual harassment' *Journal of Management* 13 (1) 149-161.

Rubenstein, M. (1988). *The Dignity of Women at Work*. Luxembourg: Commission of the European Communities.

Safran, C. (1976). 'What men do to women on the job'. *Redbook*, *148*, November.

Schweiger, D.M. Ivancevich, J.M. & Power, F.R. (1987). 'Executive actions for managing human resources before and after acquisitions'. *Academy of Management Executive*, 2, 127-38.

Searby, F. (1969). 'Control of post-merger change'. *Harvard Business Review*, September-October.

Studner, P. (1989). *Super Job Search*. London: Mercury Books.

Super, D. (1957). *The Psychology of Careers*. New York: Harper and Row.

References

Torrington, D. & Cooper, C.L. (1990). 'How to create a new life after 50'. *Sunday Times*, 9 December 1990.

UGT (General Union of Workers) (1987). *Investigacion sobre discriminacion y acaso sexual femenino en el puesto de trabajo*. Madrid.

Unger, H. (1986). 'The people trauma of major mergers'. *Journal of Industrial Management* (Canada), *10*, 17 April.

University of Groningen (1986). *Ongewensta Intimiteiten Op Het Werk*. The Netherlands.

US Merit Systems Protection Board (1980). *Sexual Harassment of Federal Workers: Is it a problem?* Washington DC: US Government Printing Office.

US Merit Systems Protection Board (1988). *Sexual Harassment of Federal Workers: An Update*. Washington DC: US Government Printing Office.

Walsh, J.P. (1988). 'Top management turnover following mergers and acquisitions'. *Strategic Management Journal*, *9*, 173-83.

Warr, P.B. (1982). 'A national study of non-financial employment commitment'. *Journal of Occupational Psychology*, *51* (2), 183-96.

Warr, P.B. (1987). *Work, Unemployment and Mental Health*. Oxford: Oxford University Press.

Woman Against Sexual Harassment (WASH), 242 Pentonville Road, London, N1 9UN.

Chapter 6 – Home and Work

Alpert, D. & Culbertson, A. (1987). 'Daily hassles and coping strategies of dual-earner and non-dual-earner women'. *Psychology of Women Quarterly*, *11*, 359-66.

Beutell, N.J. & Greenhaus, J.H. (1983). 'Integration of home and non-home roles: Women's conflict and coping behaviour'. *Journal of Applied Psychology*, *68*, 43-8.

Campbell-Moore, B. (1988). *Successful Women: Angry Men*. London: Arrow.

Cooper, C.L., Cooper, R.D. & Eaker, L.D. (1988). *Living with Stress*. London: Penguin Books.

Cooper, C.L. & Marshall, J. (1979). *Executive Under Pressure*. London: Macmillan.

Gilbert, L.A., Holohan, C.K. & Manning, L. (1981). 'Coping with conflict between professional and maternal roles'. *Family Relations*, 319-426.

Hall, T. (1972). 'A model of coping with role conflict: the role behaviours of college-educated women'. *Administrative Science Quarterly*, *1* (7), 471-86.

Hall, F.S. & Hall, T. (1980). *The Two-Career Couple*. Massachusetts: Addison-Wesley.

Handy, C. (1987). 'The family: help or hindrance'. In Cooper, C.L. and Payne, R, (eds.), *Stress at Work*. London: John Wiley & Sons, 107-23.

Ivancevich, J.M. & Matteson, M.T. (1980). *Stress at Work*. Illinois: Scott, Foresman & Co.

Lewis, S. & Cooper, C.L. (1989). *Career Couples*. London: Unwin Hyman.

Maples, M. (1981). 'Dual career marriages: elements for potential success'. *Personnel & Guidance Journal*, September, 19-23.

Watts, M. & Cooper, C.L. (1992). *Relax: Dealing with Stress*. London: BBC Books.

Index

role 83-5
task/achievement 85-6
curricula vitae (C.V.s)
    155-6, 159-61

Daily Express 183
Daily Mirror 166
deadlines 18, 20, 26, 37,
    39, 55
delegation 21, 36, 38-9,
    48, 52, 56, 71, 179
disorganization 39-41
divorce 12, 24

Elizabeth I, Queen 35
Employment Protection
    (Consolidation) Act
    146
Equal Opportunities
    Commission 138, 146
Europe 2, 3, 24, 25, 119,
    136, 138, 139, 183,
    184
European Community 2,
    3, 105, 140
exercise 10, 25, 33, 102,
    162
Exxon 163

Fijutsu 117
financial services 121
Finland 12
France 183
Frost, Robert 134

GEC 117
Germany 139, 183
Getty 131

Goethe, J. W. 162
Goldwyn, Sam 70
Guatemala 164
Guinness 163

Hardy, Peter 149
health 1, 12, 14, 61-4,
    104-5, 130, 134, 136,
    141, 152, 162
  blood pressure 8, 9, 10,
    12, 16
  heart disease 2, 4, 6, 9,
    10-1, 12, 14, 16, 17,
    20, 50, 77
  lung cancer 152
  see also alcohol,
    exercise, obesity,
    smoking
Heller, Joseph 65, 74
Hill, Professor Anita 145
holidays 55-6

ICI 31
ICL 117, 190
identity 120, 150-1
industrial disputes 1, 16
Industrial Relations Survey
    59
industry 1, 153-4
  brewing 117
  engineering 117
  manufacturing 117, 153
  mining 185
  steel 185
International Management
    Group 90
Italy 183

PROBLEM PEOPLE AT WORK
– and how to deal with them

Marilyn Wheeler

Most people in the workplace just want to get on with their jobs – but there are always a few who seem to be quite impossible to deal with: bullies, blamers, moaners, procrastinators and the downright bad-tempered. If you know how to treat them properly, however, you can solve the problems they cause. The aim of this book is not to change difficult people, but to change the way they behave to others.

It deals chapter by chapter with the most common types of problem people at work, and provides strategies for dealing successfully with their tiresome behaviour.

Marilyn Wheeler runs her own management consultancy based in Los Angeles, offering seminars and training to major corporations in the US and overseas.

£8.99 (pbk)
ISBN 0-7126-5872-6

EVERYTHING IS NEGOTIABLE

Gavin Kennedy

This bestselling business classic proves that getting a better deal is always possible. It shows how to handle every type of negotiation, from the big stake deal such as a new house or a long-term contract, to smaller, more routine ones like having a car mended or buying a TV. It includes a section on negotiating overseas.

There are special self-assessment tests in each chapter; as readers progress through the book their negotiating skills, and their scores, should improve dramatically.

If you assume that nothing is negotiable unless the other party indicates otherwise, you are missing opportunities to make better deals.

Professor Gavin Kennedy teaches at Heriot-Watt University in Edinburgh, Scotland. His consultancy Negotiate Ltd runs negotiating workshops and seminars in the UK and worldwide.

£5.99 (pbk)
ISBN 0 09 998070 3

MAVERICK!
The success story behind the world's most unusual workplace

Ricardo Semler

Maverick! is one of the most unusual books about business that you'll ever read. Ricardo Semler inherited his family company, Semco – Brazilian manufacturers of marine pumps, industrial dishwashers and mining equipment – when he was aged 19. In 1980 it was on the brink of bankruptcy, but a decade later, during a period of savage recession in Brazil, it had been transformed into a rapidly growing company with profits of 10% on sales of $37 million.

This amazing turnaround was achieved by throwing out the rulebook, letting workers make the decisions previously made by their bosses, and set their own salary levels and production schedules. These changes stemmed from a series of 30 programmes designed to change the entire working environment.

Ricardo Semler is president of Semco/SA, Brazil's largest marine and food processing machinery manufacturer. His book about the company is the alltime bestselling non-fiction book in Latin America, and together with his revolutionary article "Managing Without Managers" in the *Harvard Business Review* has provoked intense discussion among senior management around the world.

£16.99 (hbk)
ISBN 0 7126 5451 8